LIBRARY OF THE EARLY CIVILIZATIONS
EDITED BY PROFESSOR STUART PIGGOTT

The First Americans

THE FIRST

THE PRE-COLUMBIAN

McGraw-Hill   Book

AMERICANS

CIVILIZATIONS

G. H. S. Bushnell

Company · New York

DESIGNED AND PRODUCED BY THAMES AND HUDSON

CONTENTS

GENERAL EDITOR'S PREFACE

The archaeological discovery of the earliest Americans, while it can hardly rival in intellectual and emotional impact the geographical discovery by Europeans of the land they inhabited, has nevertheless claims to be regarded as something more than a minor incident in world prehistory. When the discovery of the New World first took place, the presence of the contemporary inhabitants immediately posed the most awkward questions. Were they the progeny of Shem, of Ham or of Japhet? And if they could not be fitted in as descendants of one of the three founding fathers of the human race, the still more awful problem loomed ahead—were they human at all? With compromise, ingenuity and a quietly waning belief in the absolute authority of Moses in matters of anthropology, the question was evaded, solved or reduced to a no-problem, but only to be replaced by another, this time real, and capable of rational elucidation by archaeological means.

With the development of the study of prehistoric man in the Old World, the chronological and cultural status of early man in the New naturally presented itself as an important problem. Even before Boucher de Perthes, it seems, the possibility of the high antiquity of man in the Americas, even going back to the Quaternary period, had been mooted; but alas, when direct evidence first seemed to become available, hoaxes and misunderstood interpretations of genuine finds bedevilled matters in America as in Europe. The stone implements from the Trenton gravels were genuine enough, but their geological context was not Quaternary, as claimed at the time, but recent; the Calaveras skull, assigned to the Pliocene, no less, was a modern Indian specimen planted in a mine-shaft—circumstances improved upon by Bret Harte when he made the 'oldest primate' announce

> 'Which my name is Bowers, and my crust was busted
> Falling down a shaft in Calaveras County'.

This was in 1886, and soon geology and archaeology emerged in a sound interdisciplinary combination to tackle the problem of the first Americans,

7

with the result, as Dr Bushnell demonstrates in this book, that today we can construct a reasonably coherent story, if only in outline. But this story, although much of its background was worked out some time ago, has only been put on a sound chronological basis within the last decade or so, thanks entirely to radiocarbon dating. While this method has proved of enormous value to Old World prehistory, to the New World it has brought chronological salvation. Without it, dates could scarcely be computed with any confidence much before a time contemporary with the early Middle Ages of Europe; today we can state that, as Dr Bushnell puts it, 'the earliest dated signs of man in America are at about 9500 BC'. Throughout the non-literate American past, into the conditional literacy of later Middle America, and beyond the point of the first European contact, C-14 dates have given us a chronological framework which each new determination strengthens.

The detailed interpretation of the results of radiocarbon assay has been constantly under discussion since Libby devised the method. Radiocarbon 'years' now seem to be units not necessarily synchronous at all times in the past with solar years. But this does not prevent us from making valid comparisons between happenings in the Old and New Worlds in broad terms, or when both are dated by the same C-14 process. Our first hunting and gathering societies in the Americas, about 9500 BC, are contemporary with the earliest emergence of agricultural techniques in the ancient Near East, almost justifying Sir Thomas Browne's well-known phrase, 'The Huntsmen are up in *America*, and they are already past their first sleep in *Persia*'. But in Mexico, between 5000 and 3000 BC, maize was first cultivated, as wheat and barley were in Europe at the same time; the earliest Olmec ceremonial centres on the Gulf Coast were being constructed before and at the time of the building of the Parthenon, and within the time span of the Hallstatt and earlier La Tène cultures in barbarian Europe. The Classic period of Maya civilization extended over a period parallel with that from the later Roman Empire to the European Dark Ages at the end of Charlemagne's Empire.

Apart from the intrinsic interest of the early American civilizations, and the power and range of their art, they provide a fascinating counterpart to what happened in the Old World. By the tenth millennium BC America is first being colonized by man as a result of the arrival across the Bering Strait of emigrants from North-East Asia in an Ultimate Palaeolithic or Mesolithic state of culture. Old and New Worlds start, from that time, independent technological and social developments from a common cultural level. Both continents then begin to show areas of innovation and areas of conserving cultures: Middle America goes with the Near East and China in precocious advance, while in the Archaic and Woodlands cultures of North America we see the counterparts of much that characterizes the Eurasiatic Mesolithic and Neolithic. But then divergencies appear, equally fascinating and illuminating. The absence of suitable mammals as potential domesticates, especially for draught purposes, must be linked with the non-invention of the wheel in the New World; iron-working did not develop; the ceremonial centre became the social focus rather than the city of the Old World tradition. Forms of writing are invented, however, independently on both sides of the Atlantic. The archaeology of Ancient America affords us, in effect, a 'control' situation against which to place the sequence of social and technological developments among communities in Europe, Asia, Africa or Australia, and demonstrates the variety of solutions to the problems of subsistence, organization, and the control of nature and natural resources that can be made by that most variable and adaptable of animals, man.

STUART PIGGOTT

INTRODUCTION

Five years ago I attempted to survey the most significant stages in the beginning and growth of civilization in America in a single chapter. This has been expanded here to cover more ground, and it has been revised to take account of new discoveries in a very active field. After a general account of the earliest signs of human activity throughout the continent, attention has had to be concentrated on the areas where the highest civilizations developed, namely Mesoamerica comprising Mexico and the adjacent countries to the south and east where the Maya civilization flourished, and the Central Andes comprising Peru and Bolivia. The area which lies between them has been briefly surveyed, although it did not rise to the same heights, because it played a part in the growth of their civilizations by reason of its position. Apart from the early stages, North America and much of South America have been omitted. Interesting though they are in themselves, there is some justification for their omission because they lay on the margins of the nuclear areas, and had little effect on them, though there were considerable currents of influence in the other direction.

When Columbus arrived in American waters in 1492, American culture was like a range of mountains, rising from lowlands in Alaska and Tierra del Fuego, through the foothills of the United States and Chile, to the great twin peaks of Mesoamerica and Peru, with lesser heights over the intervening Central and South American areas. In the peak areas, man had reached a high state of culture, and the Inca and the more advanced Mexicans possessed most of the features generally regarded as marking a civilized community. At the other extreme were the Eskimo in the north and the tribes of Tierra del Fuego in the south, but though their resources were meagre and their cultures simple, they were highly adapted to their harsh surroundings and must have lived in them for a long time.

The high cultures had many features which the Spaniards could understand. There were hierarchical states, whose rulers lived in considerable splendour, fine buildings, specialist craftsmen, and a religion which played a dominant part in the lives of the people, though its practices were far from being such as they could approve of. On the other hand, the civilizations they encountered lacked iron, the wheel, the plough and the alphabet, and the invaders must have wondered to find a civilized people without those things which they took for granted in their own life, and who had moreover neither horses, cattle, sheep nor pigs, and who ate strange plants. This state of affairs had taken a long time to develop, and it is the purpose of this book to outline its growth.

G. H. S. B.

CHRONOLOGY

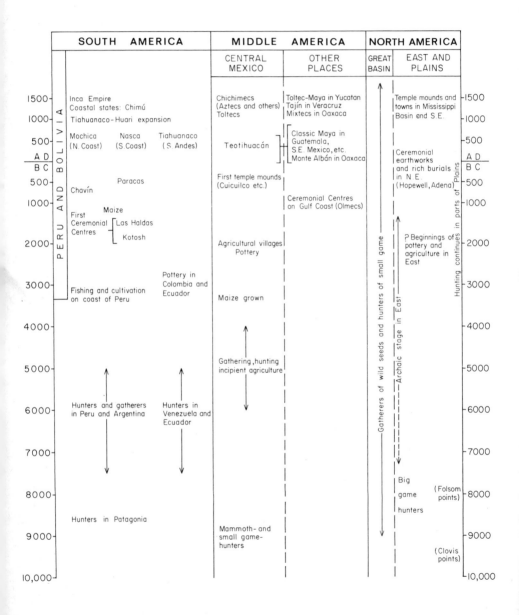

| | SOUTH AMERICA | | | MIDDLE AMERICA | | NORTH AMERICA | |
				CENTRAL MEXICO	OTHER PLACES	GREAT BASIN	EAST AND PLAINS
1500	Inca Empire			Chichimecs (Aztecs and others)	Toltec-Maya in Yucatan, Tajín in Veracruz		Temple mounds and towns in Mississippi
1000	Coastal states: Chimú Tiahuanaco-Huari expansion			Toltecs	Mixtecs in Oaxaca		Basin and S.E.
500	Mochica (N.Coast)	Nasca (S.Coast)	Tiahuanaco (S. Andes)	Teotihuacán	Classic Maya in Guatemala, S.E. Mexico, etc.		Ceremonial earthworks
A D					Monte Albán in Oaxaca		and rich burials
B C							in N.E.
500	Chavín	Paracas		First temple mounds (Cuicuilco etc.)			(Hopewell, Adena)
1000	First Ceremonial Centres	Maize			Ceremonial Centres on Gulf Coast (Olmecs)		
2000		Las Haldas, Kotosh		Agricultural villages Pottery			? Beginnings of pottery and agriculture in East
3000	Fishing and cultivation on coast of Peru	Pottery in Colombia and Ecuador		Maize grown			
4000							
5000				Gathering, hunting incipient agriculture			
6000	Hunters and gatherers in Peru and Argentina	Hunters in Venezuela and Ecuador					
7000							
8000							Big game hunters (Folsom points)
9000	Hunters in Patagonia			Mammoth- and small game-hunters			
10,000							(Clovis points)

(Left margin: PERU AND BOLIVIA)

(Great Basin column, vertical text: Gatherers of wild seeds and hunters of small game)

(East and Plains column, vertical text: Archaic stage in East — Hunting continues in parts of Plains)

CHAPTER ONE

Early Man Before 5000 BC

The coming of man to the New World was largely controlled by climate and geography. The only way by which he could have come was the Bering Strait region, and before boats were invented he would have had to cross on dry land. Between approximately 25000 and 9000 BC, north-east Asia and Alaska were connected by a wide plain, which had become land when sea-level was lowered by the locking-up of a great deal of water in the ice-sheets of the last stage, called the Wisconsin, of the quaternary ice age. It has recently been determined that Canada and parts of the northern United States were covered by a thick ice-sheet from coast to coast between about 18000 BC and a mild period some time between 10000 and 9000 BC when a corridor opened just east of the Rocky Mountains. Alaska, which remained free from ice, was really part of Asia and man could have colonized it at any time after about 25000 BC, but after 18000 BC his way south was blocked for over eight thousand years. The mild period after this was followed by a colder one from about 9000 to 8000 BC, after which the climate began to warm up, bringing the Ice Age to an end. After a cool, wet beginning there was a period warmer than the present, lasting from about 5000 to 2000 BC. This was associated with desert conditions in western North

Ref. 1

1 The spear-thrower is a device for increasing the range of a spear. Invented in Palaeolithic times, it is still in use by Eskimos and Australian aborigines (seen here)

America, while the East was probably warm and wet, like the contemporary Atlantic period in western Europe. After 2000 BC conditions approached those of the present time.

When, between 8000 and 5000 BC, the climate became milder and the oceans filled up, any new migrations would normally have been by boat, although it is still possible to cross on the ice in winter. It is not known when boats were first used to cross the Bering Strait, but they were known by the seventh millennium BC in northern Europe, so they could have been used here at an early date.

The earliest dated signs of man in America are at about 9500 BC, when hunters were roaming parts of the United States in pursuit of large mammals, much in the manner of the ancient hunters of Europe and Asia. It is possible that they came south from Alaska through the newly opened corridor in the ice, but nothing very like their specialized spear-heads and other stone tools has yet been found from this time in north-east Asia, so it has been suggested that they may have come before the way was closed by ice, between 25000 and 18000 BC, and that likely ancestors for them and their material culture may yet be found somewhere in America. Persistent claims have indeed been made for signs of the presence of man at dates older than 20000 BC, but they are far from being likely ancestors; there are fires which man may, or may not, have lit – animals he may, or may not, have killed – and crudely flaked stone objects, some of them natural and others which he might have made at any time up to the Spanish Conquest or later. By weight of numbers these finds have been built up into an impression of probability, but the idol has feet of clay, and a single well-authenticated instance would do more to support it than any number of doubtful finds. Within the last few years a very extensive excavation has been undertaken at

Tule Springs, Nevada, a site which is one of those most frequently cited as dating from before 20000 BC, but it was found that the only signs of human occupation dated from about 9000 BC and were sparse at that.

The early hunters of the tenth millennium BC and later have left their traces mainly in places where they killed their prey, but a few temporary camp sites have been found. Characteristic of these early hunter sites are various types of beautifully flaked stone point, in some cases in contact with the bones of victims. It has generally been assumed that these were the heads of spears thrown by means of the spear-thrower, a device still used by the Eskimos and the Australian aborigines, but doubts have been expressed about the effectiveness of these rather fragile objects in piercing the hides of animals like mammoths. It has even been suggested that the points were knives used for skinning and cutting up the carcasses, although obvious knives have also been found. Doubtless the main means of hunting these animals was to stampede them over a cliff or into a swamp or pound, or drive them to exhaustion, but stone-tipped spears could have been a powerful instrument in causing the stampede and they could have been thrust into vital points when the animal was tired or bogged down. Spear-throwers were certainly in use by about 7000 BC, and were probably introduced by the first arrivals.

Ill. 1

The earliest unquestioned dated finds, of about 9500 BC, are associated with a type of point called Clovis, and these have been found with the remains of mammoth and horse. Man was hunting mammoth in the Valley of Mexico in the next millennium. Many finds, dating from between 8000 and 5000 BC, when the climate was improving, show that the hunters were ranging over a wide area of the United States from the Great Plains eastward, killing mainly an extinct species of bison. They used many varieties of stone point, of which one, the Folsom point,

Ill. 2

Ref. 2

Ill. 2

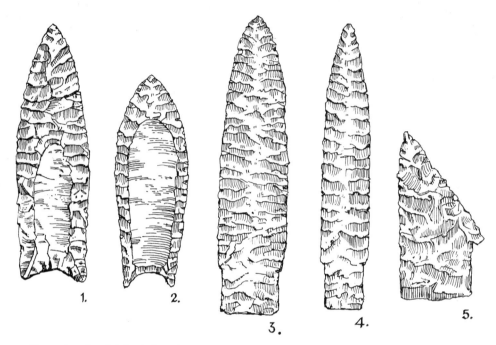

2 Examples of early North American stone artefacts. 1. Clovis point; 2. Folsom point; 3. Scotts-bluff point; 4. Eden point; 5. Cody knife. These and many other varieties of point are found particularly at kill sites. Cruder tools such as choppers, knives and scrapers, as well as points, occur at camp sites

Ill. 2

is a household word in American archaeology. It is identified by a longitudinal flake scar on each face, a device to assist hafting, which is present but less developed on the Clovis point. Two other types, the Scottsbluff and Eden points, are sometimes found together with an artifact suitable for butchering called the Cody knife. It could not be expected that the hunters lived entirely on big game, and finds on camp sites and in rock shelters show that they were glad to catch or collect anything which could be eaten, such as seeds, plants, rabbits, snakes and snails.

While the big-game hunters lived in the Plains and parts of the East, people who lived rather differently

3 Sandal made of shredded sage-bush rope. The sole is made by close twining, and the flap which covers the front of the foot by open twining with a thinner cord of the same material. From Fort Rock Cave, Oregon, where many were found, this is probably the oldest known footwear, c. 7000 BC

occupied other parts of North America. West of the Rocky Mountains, in the Great Basin, Washington, Oregon and California the gathering of wild seeds and plants was more important than hunting, and some of the larger animals, such as the extinct bison, were rare or absent. Ground sloth, horse and camel, all of which later became extinct, were hunted in some places, but in others only forms which still survive, like mountain sheep, ante-lopes and duck. Fishing was possible only in a few places, but the salmon run was exploited at The Dalles, Oregon, where the Columbia River enters the gorge through the Cascade Range. Some of the most important finds come from dry caves, where materials normally perishable are preserved, and these include rope sandals and specialized types of twined basketry, which are still being made in the West. These people are believed to have been in the area by 9000 B C, and by 7000 B C some of them were exploiting all the meagre resources of a harsh environment in much the same way as their successors continued to do until about 1850. The extreme north-west of the United States may have been occupied even earlier than the west, by people who fished, collected shell-fish, and hunted deer and smaller animals using spears tipped with lanceolate stone points with a lenticular cross-section, similar to a type called Lerma in Mexico.

Long before the extinction (6000–5000 B C) of the large fauna which was hunted in the Plains and the East, caves in Illinois, Alabama and Missouri were occupied by people who lived by foraging like those of the West but under better conditions, in fact they were the forerunners of the numerous and varied groups which lived in the East during the Archaic stage between about 5000 B C and the beginnings of agriculture. The relationships between these foragers, those of the West, and the hunters is a problem which has not yet been resolved. The realization that foraging and hunting small game must have supplemented big game hunting has diminished the differences between these groups, and they may indeed have been essentially the same people. Perhaps the most reasonable explanation is that small groups came across the Bering Strait region at different times over a span of several thousand years, and adapted themselves in various ways to the widely differing conditions and resources of their new home.

Less is known of the earliest Americans in the vast area south of Mexico, which was populated from the north, although they are known to have been hunting the ground sloth and the native horse in southern Patagonia between

9000 and 8000 B C. A few stone points, found on the surface, are the only signs of their presence on their southward journey between Mexico and the Isthmus of Panama. (The famous footprints found deep in volcanic ash in Nicaragua are those of men and animals fleeing from an eruption of a much later time.) If any of them followed the coast, their remains will have been washed away by the rising sea of post-glacial times, and if they penetrated the highlands traces of them may yet be found in the caves which abound in Costa Rica and Honduras.

Finds of points and other stone implements are scattered widely in South America. Quartzite points similar to the Lerma points of Mexico and the north-west of the United States have been found in a stratified sequence in the Cave of Intihuasi in Argentina, and firmly dated at about 6000 B C. Spears tipped with these points appear to have been used for hunting deer and llamas, but seeds of wild plants were also eaten, since stones with polished facets, which were produced by use in grinding them up, are also found. Similar points are found at El Jobo in Venezuela and Lauricocha in highland Peru, but firm dates for them have not been obtained, although the underlying horizon at Lauricocha, with deer-bone spearpoints and crude stone tools has been dated about 7500 B C. Obsidian tools, such as knives, burins and various types of spear-point, some of which compare closely with points found in the lowest horizon in southern Patagonia, were left by hunters at El Inga, not far from Quito in highland Ecuador.

The central part of the desert coast of Peru has recently (1963) yielded some surprising discoveries, namely an assemblage of stone tools, about which little has yet been published, dated about 8500 B C in the Chillon Valley, and a series of groups of stone implements – points, scrapers, grinding-stones and mortars – left by people who occupied patches of vegetation watered by sea mists during the winter months. They hunted deer and gathered grass seeds and snails during the winter, and moved elsewhere, perhaps to the mountains, during the summer. This went on from about 6000 BC, perhaps before, until increased activity in the cool Humboldt Current between 3000 and 2000 BC reduced the moisture so that much of the vegetation dried up and the people either moved or adopted other ways of life, but small patches of vegetation survive even now, and there are still winter mists to give an idea of the conditions long ago. The changes in the Humboldt Current brought increased fish life, and permanent fishing villages, practising a limited amount of plant cultivation, were established at about the same time.

There is, then, plenty of evidence for the presence of hunting and gathering peoples in many parts of South America at an early date, and the remains in Patagonia suggest that they arrived before 9000 BC.

CHAPTER TWO

The Rise of the Farmers

North America

About 5000 BC begins the story of the development of permanent settlements in favoured spots, although it was not until the full development of agriculture that they became widespread.

Even when they did, it must not be imagined that hunting and gathering ceased; the buffalo-hunters of the Great Plains, the acorn-gatherers of California, the Fuegians and the Eskimos remind us that these ways of making a living have lasted into our own times.

In those parts of the eastern United States where the climate of the Altithermal period was warm and wet are found sites which show that people were able to live for considerable lengths of time in one place, or at any rate to return to it at frequent intervals over a long period. The remains found on these sites are far from uniform, except in the things they lack, such as pottery, earthworks, substantial buildings, and evidence of agriculture, but they are at a generally similar cultural level, called by archaeologists the Archaic stage.

Along rivers in Kentucky and Tennessee are mounds built up over a long period from the discarded shells of freshwater mussels, the regular source of food which enabled the people to remain there. Among their possessions

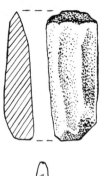

4, 5 Archaic artifacts from the eastern U.S.A. *Left, centre:* Bone needle *above* and *below:* Stone adze and gouge for wood-working. *Above,* a banner-stone, a weight used for balancing a spear-thrower

Ill. 4

Ill. 5

Ill. 6

were ground stone axes for wood working, stone pestles for grinding wild seeds and berries, and spear-throwers of bone and antler with which they hunted the deer whose bones are found in the shell-heaps. In the forests of the north-east, and in and around New York and New England, were bands of people who were probably less settled, although their rubbish-heaps show that a few spots were, if not semi-permanent settlements, at least favourite camping places. They had stone slabs, mortars, mullers and pestles for grinding acorns and other plant food, bone hooks and gorges for fishing, stone-tipped spears for hunting, and stone adzes for wood working, to which were added later stone gouges, weights called banner-stones for attachment to spear-throwers, bone needles, soapstone vessels and other things.

In both areas the dead were buried, with grave goods of various kinds, in the refuse-dumps, and in some cases in the north-east they were accompanied by powdered red ochre, a dog or a second human skull. Turtle-shell rattles, bone flutes and whistles, and necklaces of shell beads and animal teeth give an indication of interests outside the daily quest for food, and there is evidence of contacts with peoples far away, in the shape of tools and weapons beaten out of native copper from Lake Superior, and

6 Three spear-heads beaten out of native copper, which comes from the Lake Superior region. Archaic stage, eastern U.S.A.

shells from Florida. (This does not imply a knowledge of true metal working, which was quite unknown in America until much later. The copper was treated as a malleable stone.) When agriculture began in this region is uncertain, and the Archaic stage is assumed to have ended about 1500 BC with the coming of pottery and other features previously lacking.

It is always difficult to detect the beginnings of agriculture among archaeological remains, and in a wet climate it may be impossible. Agriculture does not necessarily coincide with the introduction of pottery and other 'neolithic' features as in Britain or in other parts of the Old World, in fact it is known that ground stone tools were used in North America long before, and that in at least two areas pottery was introduced long after. When man eventually learnt how to cultivate plants, it was the chief factor in enabling him to produce a supply of food steady enough to let him settle down in permanent villages, but it took a long time. In the Old World the process has been called the Neolithic Revolution, but in America at least it was so slow that this is a misnomer. In the Old World, the domestication of animals played a very important part, alongside that of plants, but its contribution can be ignored in America in the early stages everywhere and in some places altogether, so that wild animals remained an important source of protein food. What is known of llama and alpaca domestication in historic times indicates that these animals were valued more for their hair than their meat. It is unlikely that cultivation developed only in one place in America, because the first stumbling steps in the domestication of different plants appear to have been taken in different places, for example some species of beans, cotton, cucurbits and tobacco which were domesticated in Mesoamerica were different from the Peruvian species of those genera.

Ill. 12

Mexico

Ref. 4

After a good deal of search an area has been found in highland Mexico which is theoretically suitable for the domestication of plants and also provides dry caves in which perishable remains are preserved. Here in the Tehuacán Valley in the State of Puebla, a record of continuous human occupation from the earliest times to the Spanish Conquest has been found. Starting with perhaps a dozen to twenty-five hunters and foragers about 9000 B C the population increased forty-fold by the time permanent agricultural villages were established about 2000 B C. The earliest peoples, who were roughly contemporary with the mammoth-hunters of the Valley of Mexico and possibly part of the same group, obtained most of their meat from jack rabbits, birds and turtles, and between about 6700 and 5000 B C they seemed to have lived mainly by collecting wild plants such as beans and amaranth which they seasoned with chile peppers. They lived in caves in the rainy season and camped out in the dry. Judging by the size of the seeds they had begun to cultivate a squash and perhaps alligator pears. They left polished stone mortars, pestles and grinding-stones in their caves, showing that they ground seeds for use as food. Maize pollen occurs in the cave deposits and towards the end of the period a few minute chewed wild maize cobs have been found. These are the earliest fruits of a plant which under cultivation became the mainstay of all the great civilizations of ancient America, for there is no plant which produces beneficial mutations more abundantly in the hand of man. Between 5000 and 3500 BC the population of the valley increased to about ten times its original size, and cultivation increased, but even so only about ten per cent of the plant food came from cultivated plants. To those already grown were added the common bean and a second variety of squash, while a few rather larger maize cobs show that the selection of improved strains was beginning, although the wild plant survived and continued to do so until about AD 250, when it became extinct. In the next stage there was a marked change, and by 3000 BC about thirty per cent of the plants eaten were cultivated. Maize was improving rapidly, and the cultivated cobs, which were considerably larger, made up about half the total number. A related grass from a neighbouring area crossed with the maize to form a hybrid called *teosinte*, and this in turn back-crossed with maize to produce new varieties. People ceased to live in the caves in the wet season but made temporary camps there in the dry, spending a good deal of time near their fields in the valley in the wet summer season. They may have begun to construct permanent pit-house villages about 3000 BC, but it seems more probable that permanent villages came with predominant agriculture between 2500 and 2000 BC. In other parts of Mexico permanent villages have not been proved to have existed before about 1500 BC. Stone jars and bowls were in use long before, but it was not until about 2300 BC that the first pottery, in form very like the stone bowls and very poor in quality, was made in the Valley of Tehuacán.

Two other groups of cave dwellings have been studied in north-east Mexico. Although this was a backward area the same kind of development from food gathering to agriculture has been observed, but it is of interest here chiefly because more than one variety of maize was cultivated at an early date. In one area, the Sierra Madre, is found a type related to the earliest maize from Tehuacán, which is also found in an early horizon (possibly before 3500 BC) in Bat Cave, New Mexico, and which is related to a surviving strain called Chapalote. In the other, the Sierra de Tamaulipas, is found a different sort related to the living strain Nal-Tel. There is a strong suggestion that these two varieties were domesticated in different centres.

The early settled farming villages of the Valley of Mexico have been taken as our example of the next stage because a good deal is known about them. Although they were not the first, they were occupied by 1000 BC and perhaps before. At that time there was a great lake in the valley. On its margins were reed-covered swamps which gave cover for game, and the surrounding hills were clothed with forests of pine and evergreen oak. At seven thousand feet it had a temperate climate, and it was good country to live in. The people settled first on the dry ground beyond the swamps and eventually formed a group of villages at El Arbillo, Tlatilco, Zacatenco, Copilco, Cuicuilco and other places, some of which were occupied until about 100 BC. We do not yet know where these people came from before they colonized the valley. They cut the scrub with stone axes and probably burnt it, so clearing fields in which they grew maize, beans and squash, which they planted with digging-sticks. In the woods they hunted deer, peccaries and other animals, with obsidian-tipped spears and perhaps bow and arrow. The lake, the rivers and the swamps provided them with fish, frogs, tortoises and wild fowl, which they caught with net and trap. They collected roots and tubers, prickly pears and other wild fruits, rushes to make mats and reeds

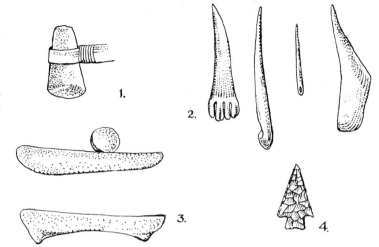

7 Artifacts of the first farmers in the Valley of Mexico. 1. Polished stone axe-head and method of hafting; 2. Three bone awls and a needle; 3. Two querns, one with a stone muller; 4. Obsidian projectile point

and grass for thatching their houses, which were simple rectangles of mud-plastered cane. They ground their maize on rectangular or oval grinding-stones; they cut up their hides and meat with obsidian knives, and they had bone awls and needles.

Ill. 7

They were skilled potters, making their vessels by hand-modelling or coiling, because like all American peoples they did not use the wheel. Their commonest vessels were jars, bowls and tripod bowls, decorated in the earlier stages chiefly by incision with little painting, but paint became more frequent later; finally a polychrome of red designs outlined with white on a buff ground was sometimes used. Judging from the figurines, the women wore no clothes in the earliest part of the period, though some are shown wearing short skirts later on, and at all times some of them had ornaments such as ear-plugs, nose-rings, necklaces, anklets and turbans, and some painted their bodies with designs in various colours. The men are shown wearing only a brief loin-cloth. Such clothing as they had was woven from local vegetable fibres such as yucca, and in the later stages from cotton brought from lower altitudes. They knew nothing of any metals.

Ill. 9

Ill. 8

At first the only indications of religion are the numerous female figurines of pottery, possibly used in ceremonies

Ill. 8

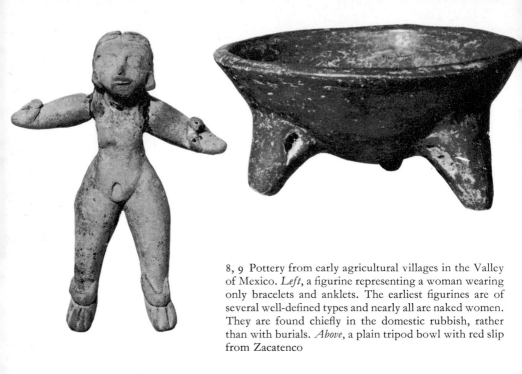

8, 9 Pottery from early agricultural villages in the Valley of Mexico. *Left*, a figurine representing a woman wearing only bracelets and anklets. The earliest figurines are of several well-defined types and nearly all are naked women. They are found chiefly in the domestic rubbish, rather than with burials. *Above*, a plain tripod bowl with red slip from Zacatenco

to promote the fertility of the crops or in curing ceremonies, but by about 600 B C shrines raised on platforms or mounds had begun to be built. These were the fore-runners of the prominent pyramids built later in the same region, but it is now known that more imposing structures were built even earlier in the Olmec region on the Gulf Coast. The best example in the valley is at Cuicuilco; it is a terraced circular structure of clay reinforced with large stones, which in its final state, after an enlargement, had four stages, and was approached by ramps, perhaps stairways, from east and west. There was a clay altar painted red on the top, presumably sheltered by a thatched roof. Figurines in the shape of an aged man representing the god of fire appear at the same time.

Ill. 10

The occupation of Cuicuilco, the neighbouring village of Copilco, and other sites was brought to an end by an eruption of the volcano Xitle, which overwhelmed them some two thousand years ago.

10 Reconstruction of the circular pyramid and shrine at Cuicuilco, Valley of Mexico, as it probably appeared shortly before the eruption of Xitle that buried it. It is still partly buried under the Pedregal, the lava flow on the outskirts of Mexico City

Peru

Cultivation began early on the Peruvian coast, in limited areas in valleys where there was sufficient water, and its special interest here is that in its beginnings it must have been independent from Mexican centres. The earliest cultivated plants were lima beans and cucurbits (squashes), but they belong to different varieties from the Mexican ones. Maize did not appear until very late; the exact date is uncertain but it seems to have been present between 1400 and 1200 BC, and it may possibly have been domesticated independently in the Peruvian highlands. It was not until the local type crossed with a strain introduced from Mesoamerica about the ninth century BC that it began to be an important source of food. In all the earlier coastal villages the people lived chiefly on the harvest of the sea, sea-lions, fish and shell-fish, and it was the steady food supply from this source that made permanent settlement possible. So important was it that some settlements

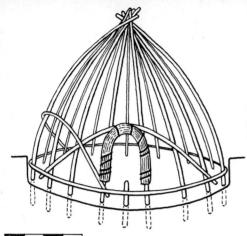

11 Hut with cane framework (*top*) covered with sedge, with the floor slightly sunk. Fourth millennium BC, from Chilca, 67 km. south of Lima, south coast of Peru. (After Donnan)

12 Llamas in highland Peru, near Cuzco. There are ▷ two forms of domesticated cameloid in the Andean region, the llama and the alpaca, and two wild forms, the guanaco and the vicuña

1 m.

were built in waterless areas where sea food was abundant.

It has already been indicated that cultivation on a small scale began between 3000 and 2000 BC in the central part of the coast. In the south it began earlier, and burials associated with horticulture have been reported near Paracas and dated about 6900 BC, but no other details are yet available. If this is confirmed it will be the oldest known instance of cultivation anywhere in America. There are several instances of the cultivation of beans and squash between 4000 and 3000 BC. In one village a well-preserved beehive hut built of cane covered with sedge was found; dated about 3400 BC, this is the earliest known artificial shelter in Peru, and it is remarkably like huts used in the neighbourhood within living memory. In one cemetery the dead were buried wrapped in the skins of cameloids, probably vicuñas, which live in the high Andes, so there were contacts with that area. In most

Ref. 5
Ill. 11
Ref. 6

Ill. 12

instances twined sedge mats were used for this purpose,
which concerns us because this method was used later for
making cotton textiles with elaborate patterns.

After 3000 B C many settlements were established along
the coast. They are distinguished from their predecessors
by the cultivation of cotton, and from their successors
after about 1200 B C by the lack of pottery. The cotton
was used, sometimes in combination with bast fibres, for
making textiles by hand without the aid of a loom, chiefly
by the twining process. This is not an easy medium for
producing patterns, but the weavers managed, by means
of warp transpositions, to work sophisticated designs
such as double-headed snakes and fish, birds of prey with
fish inside them, and highly stylized human beings, the
chief expression of the earliest Peruvian art, which had its
effect on the later styles. The people appear mostly to have
lived in single-roomed houses of various materials, stone

Ills 13, 14

and mud rubble, mud brick, and poles and sedge, some on the surface and some partly or wholly underground. They cooked by roasting on hot stones. Some of the settlements were of considerable size, at least in the later part of the period, and imposing temple structures have been reported, for example at Las Haldas just south of Casma, dated about 1600 B C. The early date of such constructions is supported by the discovery of an elaborate temple at Kotosh in the central highlands, before the introduction of pottery in that region which has been dated at about 1800 B C. The implication is that temple worship and a religious hierarchy developed over 600 years earlier in Peru than similar developments in Mexico.

The cultivated plants so far discussed are grown from seed, but there remains a group grown from roots or tubers which plays and has played an important part, particularly in South America. Chief among these is the

13, 14 Piece of twined cotton textile, shown with the warps running horizontally. The dyes having faded, the pattern is not apparent. The zigzag effect is due to warp displacements. The same piece is shown in *Ill. 14*. The warps were followed under a microscope, and irregularities

manioc, upon which great numbers still depend in the lowlands, and the potato in the highlands, but neither lends itself to preservation and they generally grow in places too wet to allow it. Such evidence for their presence as pottery griddles for manioc and dried potatoes (*chuño*) comes far too late in time to throw any light on the origins of the domestication of these plants, so we still depend on speculation. It was suggested some years ago that this sort of cultivation developed early in the Amazonian lowlands and spread to the high Andes, although most archaeologists have doubted that any good thing could come out of that area. The finding of sedentary pottery-using communities in the Peruvian lowlands east of the Andes at dates estimated at about 2000 BC has prompted the revival of that suggestion, but a good deal of un-certainty remains, and we may find that different tubers were domesticated in different regions as with the seed plants.

Ref. 8

plotted. This enabled the photograph to be retouched, revealing the original pattern of a condor with a snake in its stomach. The colours are reversed on the back. Preceramic period, Huaca Prieta, Chicama Valley, Peru

15 Colossal basalt head, about 8 feet high with typical Olmec features, wearing a helmet with side flaps. Originally from La Venta, Tabasco, it is now in the 'Olmec Park' at Villahermosa. Four such heads were found at La Venta, and others at other Olmec sites

CHAPTER THREE

Priests and Princes

When permanent settlements had been established in Mesoamerica and Peru, whether supported by agriculture or the sea, temples and shrines were built. The length of time which elapsed before this happened varied in different places, but recent discoveries have shortened it to a marked extent in some at least of the important centres, and complex groups of buildings, making up what are called ceremonial centres, have been shown to have existed at surprisingly early dates. There were a number of major centres of growth in Mesoamerica, but there were relationships between them which enable them to be discussed together. The course of events in Peru, however, is sufficiently distinct for it best to be treated separately.

In Mesoamerica the earliest ceremonial centres, and the hierarchy to which they belonged, arose in the tropical Gulf Coast lowlands of southern Veracruz and Tabasco, and they are given the name of Olmec. The best example, La Venta, is believed to have flourished between 1000 and 600 BC, but the Olmec art style must have been developing even earlier. Massive mounds and typical Olmec stone carvings dating from 1200 to 900 BC have recently been found at San Lorenzo, not far from La Venta. La Venta is on a low island in the swamps and its focus is an

Ref. 9

enormous pyramid with two courts adjoining it to the north along a roughly north–south axis. These are bounded by platforms and mounds, and the platforms of the northern one are crowned by palisades of natural basalt columns. Pyramids, mounds and platforms were built of clay and painted red, yellow and purple. Other features of the site are four colossal stone heads, the largest over eight feet high, with loose-lipped 'baby' faces, carved basalt monuments of various forms, caches of baby-faced figurines and celts of jade and other stones, and rectangular pits filled by layer upon layer of serpentine blocks, in one case amounting to twelve hundred tons. Three of these serpentine offerings, for so they must have been, were topped by a rectangular mosaic of serpentine and coloured sands thought to be highly stylized jaguar masks. Through all the art of the Olmec sites runs the theme of a sexless human figure with a puffy, loose-lipped face and a cleft head, generally of infantile appearance but sometimes like a snarling jaguar. Thought to be the offspring of a jaguar and a woman, these 'were-jaguars' have been interpreted as celestial rain spirits, the forebears of all the rain gods of Mesoamerica.

These tropical lowlands were the home of the Olmec culture, but its influence, as shown by the art style, extended far. There are rock carvings in El Salvador,

Ill. 15

Ill. 16

Ill. 17

16, 17 Finds from La Venta, Tabasco. *Left*, a large rectangular pavement of serpentine blocks and coloured sand representing an abstract jaguar mask. There were three such pavements at the site, covering pits filled with serpentine blocks, and they were covered with clay shortly after being laid down. *Right*, a detail of the basalt Altar 5, showing two helmeted figures carrying 'were-jaguar' babies with cleft heads

Guatemala and the Mexican State of Morelos, and some remarkable paintings have been reported in a cave in Guerrero, but far commoner are small portable objects such as carved and engraved celts and figurines of jade from Guerrero, Puebla, Morelos and the Valley of Mexico. Several sites in the last three areas have produced fragile hollow pottery figurines of Olmec style, especially Tlatilco on the outskirts of Mexico City, a village which is thought to have flourished between 800 and 300 BC, possibly starting earlier. The inhabitants must have lived in a very similar way to their neighbours at Zacatenco and the rest, but they were in some ways more sophisticated. They had different types of pottery, including finely modelled life forms like fish, armadillo and duck in polished black ware, which are real works of art. They made pottery masks representing fantastic beings, or jaguars and other animals, and one miniature example is divided vertically in the middle, one half showing a face with protruding tongue and the other a skull. They had new types of figurine: women with children, dancing girls, masked magicians or priests, and even a man equipped to play a ball-game of which we shall hear more later. They had fine Olmec figurines of jade. There are many signs of jaguar worship, and some evidence of human sacrifice to supply attendants for the dead.

Ref. 10

Ill. 20

Ill. 19
Ill. 18

Ills 21, 22

Ill. 23
Ill. 24

18, 19 *Above*, part of a cemetery at the Olmec-influenced site of Tlatilco, near Mexico City, *c*. 800 to 300 BC. The burials, which have been left in place, were richly furnished with pottery vessels and figurines. There is a large hollow figurine in the foreground. Also from Tlatilco is the hollow pottery figurine of typical Olmec aspect, *left*, representing a child

20 Celt of the dark green jade generally used by the Olmecs representing an Olmec figure. The bold carving of the face accompanied by the delicate engraving of other details is typical of Olmec work

21, 22 Two vessels from Tlatilco. *Left*, a polished black bowl in the form of a fish, with traces of red colour on the rough areas. *Above*, a red-painted bowl, with geometrical figures in the brown to brownish grey colour of the ware, outlined by incision

The island at La Venta could not have supported a large population, say 150 people composed of the ruling class and their immediate attendants. It is reckoned that they were supported by some 18,000 maize-growing peasants scattered over a wide area, and a similar pattern is likely for other lowland sites. The enormous weight of serpentine, perhaps 5000 tons, and basalt must have been brought long distances, from over 100 miles to about 350, by water from the nearest sources, and this alone, quite apart from the energy put into building and rebuilding the ceremonial centre, implies an immense degree of pressure and control over the labour force by the hierarchy. It has generally been assumed that the hierarchy were priests who led the worship of the gods in the ceremonial centres and that their control over the lower orders depended on the general belief that the gods controlled the destinies of men through them, but this view has recently been challenged by some who think that control

23, 24 Double-headed figurines, figurines with two faces sharing one eye, and similar eccentricities, are typical of Tlatilco. *Left*, a pottery mask, half a face with protruding tongue and half a skull. *Right*, a pottery female figurine with two heads, with black linear painting on yellow ground

was backed by force and that the rulers were secular lords. As a corollary it has been proposed that the mechanism for the spread of the Olmec art style was a class of armed merchants like the Aztec *pochteca* over fifteen hundred years later, who traded to obtain jade and serpentine from the highland zone. However this may be, La Venta was clearly a holy place, its buildings were religious and in no way defensive, and the serpentine, basalt and jade which were brought from so far away were used for religious purposes. Even if its rulers used force, and there is no positive evidence that they did, all that we know of them indicates that their primary activity was religious. The only signs of force and violence at La Venta belong to the time of its abandonment or later, when a great deal of energy was expended in defacing over half the monuments and moving them from their places, but this appears to have been a local upheaval because Olmec culture continued and developed at Tres Zapotes.

Ref. 11

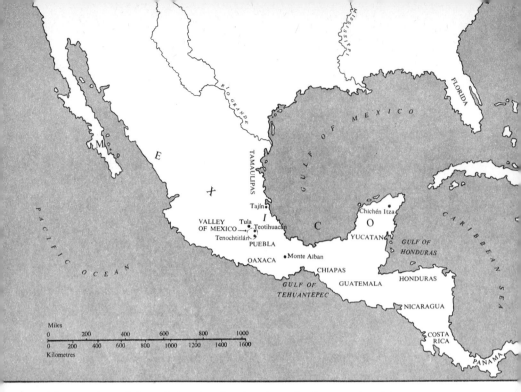

25 Mesoamerica and Central America showing the main sites mentioned in text

Oaxaca

Ill. 25
Ill. 26

Ill. 27

Olmec influence is found in a modified form in another part of Mexico, namely Oaxaca. At the great hill-top site of Monte Albán, the earliest remains in a long sequence consist of loose-limbed figures of naked men, probably corpses, carved in low relief on stone slabs found buried under later buildings. Dated between about 800 and 350 BC, some of the figures have mouths of Olmec type. They are called 'Los Danzantes' (The Dancers). They are accompanied by the oldest glyphs known in America, some of them probably denoting their names and some calendrical, but they have not been fully deciphered. Between about 350 and 100 BC there appears to have been a new wave of Olmec influence, perhaps brought about by the arrival of fresh people. A building dating from this stage at Monte Albán bears glyphs showing buildings resting

26, 27 Monte Albán, Oaxaca. *Above*, from the north end of the main plaza. Most of the buildings seen date from 100 BC to AD 950. Behind the central pyramid a building dating from Stage 2 (350–100 BC) is just visible. *Below*, a group of stone slabs bearing figures in low relief showing Olmec influence (Los Danzantes) in the south-west corner of the main plaza. They date from Stage 1 (800–350 BC)

28 Funerary urn of grey pottery representing Cocijo, the Zapotec rain god, with bifid tongue, eye-masks and large ear-spools. Monte Albán, Stage 3. 100 BC–AD 950

on an inverted head with the eyes shut, thought to represent conquered towns.

The greater part of what can now be seen at Monte Albán belongs to the next stage. There was a strong wave of influence from Teotihuacán in the Valley of Mexico, which gradually gave place after about 250 years to developments believed to be due to the local people, the ancestors of the modern Zapotecs. The hill-top was crowned with terraced platforms and pyramids of a *Ill. 26* characteristic local type, with prominent stairways, which enclose a large court with a smaller sunk one to the north of it. At the same time local styles of stone carving, pottery and wall-painting developed, the latter chiefly preserved in stone-lined tombs. The pottery is predominantly a monochrome grey ware, and one of the best-*Ill. 28* known forms is a cylindrical funerary urn on one side of which is modelled a seated figure, generally of a god, which hides it completely. Monte Albán was abandoned about AD 950, and its pottery style gradually degenerated elsewhere, disappearing about 1300.

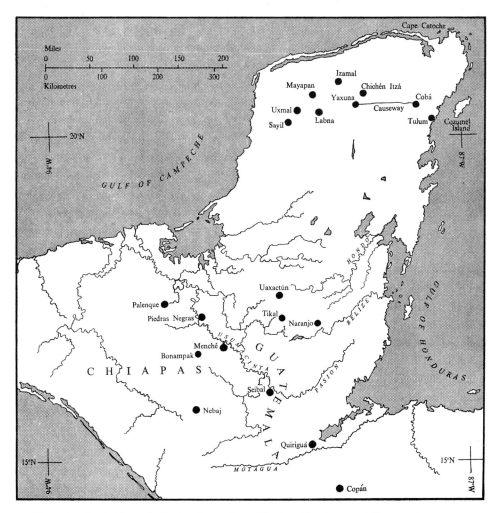

29 Maya sites in the Yucatán Peninsula, southern Mexico, Honduras and Guatemala

The Maya

The great Maya civilization is now known to have *Ill. 29* developed a good deal earlier than we used to believe. The greatest of their ceremonial centres, Tikal, was in- *Ill. 32* habited at least as early as 600 BC, and plastered masonry temples were built there between 300 and 200 BC. Uaxactún's first temples are comparable in age with those of Tikal, and the earliest activity at Kaminaljuyú, just

30 Temple I, constituting the east side of the great plaza of Tikal, Guatemala. Unlike most Maya monuments, including those on the north side of the plaza, which were reconstructed many times, this was entirely built at one time. Late Classic, *c.* AD 700. Beneath the pyramid, well north of the axis, was a very rich tomb, containing fine pottery, much jade, some delicately-engraved bones

31, 32 *Above*, is a Classic Maya jade carving, said to have been found at Teotihuacán, Central Mexico. *Right*, a jade flare in the form of part of an ear-plug, but owing to its large size (diameter 7 inches) possibly a toggle. The engraved glyphs are very early in character, suggesting a Proto-Classic or very early Classic date. Pomona, British Honduras

outside Guatemala City, can not be much later than that at Tikal. When the early horizons underlying other centres are excavated, which is no easy task, it can be expected that other and perhaps even earlier instances will be found. Although the Maya owed a good deal to other early cultures, such as that of Izapa on the tropical coastal plain of Chiapas, and through them to the Olmecs, the early horizons at Tikal have a character of their own. Maya civilization grew up until it reached a climax called the Classic period, between about AD 250 and 900, when their architecture, sculpture, pottery and other arts reached their zenith, and their calendar and the hieroglyphic writing which recorded it were fully developed. All this was dedicated to a religion of increasing elaboration.

Ill. 29
Maya remains are found in the forested lowlands of Guatemala and the adjacent areas of Mexico, British Honduras and Honduras, highland Guatemala and Chiapas, and the dry limestone plateau of Yucatán.

The Maya of the present day, who live in the same area, speak one or other of a closely related group of languages, and their ancestors doubtless did much the same; but although this sets them apart from other Mexican and Central American peoples, nevertheless Maya and non-Maya centres were not isolated from one another, because goods were exchanged far and wide between them. The great centre of Teotihuacán in Central Mexico in particular exercised strong influence in buildings, stone carving and pottery at Maya sites as far away as Tikal and
Ill. 31
Kaminaljuyú, and one of the finest Maya jades in the British Museum is reputed to have been found at Teotihuacán.

The importance of agriculture, and especially maize, in the growth of ancient American civilizations must not be forgotten. The Maya regarded the maize as the greatest gift of the creator gods, in fact it was itself a god, and to this day they address it as 'Your Grace'. In spite of the

33, 34 Wall paintings at Bonampak, Chiapas. *Above left*, the interior of one of a group of Late Classic Maya buildings showing the location of the paintings shown here. A group of richly-dressed chiefs preparing for a ceremony, and, *below*, an orchestra of rattles, tortoise-shells, trumpets and drums. The grotesque figure at the top is probably an earth monster

poverty of the soil in many places, and the continual struggle against drought in some parts and tropical vegetation in others, it gives so rich a yield that there is much spare time for the maize cultivator, and the remains show that in Classic times this was largely used in the erection and frequent reconstruction of great buildings and the maintenance of the cult. The great Maya centres have sometimes been likened to cities, but in many respects they were more akin to cathedral closes. Detailed mapping of Tikal has shown that there was a large population composed largely of specialist craftsmen immediately surrounding the ceremonial centre, but it did not approach our modern cities in density of population. The ruling

35 In another room at Bonampak the preparations in *Ill. 34* are followed by a raid in which prisoners are captured, and, in this illustration, arraigned before a high chief and some of them sacrificed

class and others who lived there must have been supported by at least as many peasants, living in small scattered settlements among their *milpas*, the clearings in which they grew their maize. Lacking draught animals and the plough, they depended entirely on human labour, and after a few years the growth of weeds, and perhaps exhaustion of the soil, meant that new *milpas* had to be laboriously cleared by cutting the timber with stone axes and burning the brushwood when dry.

The Classic period was a time of peace. The great centres were not in defensible positions and there is no sign of any attempt to fortify them. It is true that a section of the splendid Maya wall paintings at Bonampak in Chiapas depicts a fight, but from the context this appears to have been a raid on some less cultured neighbours,

Ills 33–35

36 Stucco head with a typical aristocratic Maya face from the burial ▷ chamber under the Temple of the Inscriptions, Palenque, Chiapas. Late Classic period, *c.* AD 690

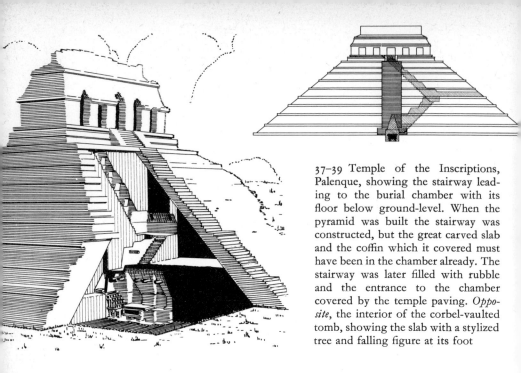

37–39 Temple of the Inscriptions, Palenque, showing the stairway leading to the burial chamber with its floor below ground-level. When the pyramid was built the stairway was constructed, but the great carved slab and the coffin which it covered must have been in the chamber already. The stairway was later filled with rubble and the entrance to the chamber covered by the temple paving. *Opposite*, the interior of the corbel-vaulted tomb, showing the slab with a stylized tree and falling figure at its foot

perhaps to obtain prisoners for sacrifice in a great ceremony. There are no signs of wars between peoples of similar status. The rulers of the various centres seem to have maintained friendly relations with the independent rulers of other large centres, forming a ruling caste among themselves. In esoteric knowledge and intellectual capacity they were doubtless far above the peasants who supported them. As in the case of the Olmecs, the nature of the ruling class is under dispute. They have generally been regarded as priests, and the monuments (stelae) showing dignified impersonal figures accompanied by long inscriptions, mostly consisting of dates, have been interpreted as marking stages in a majestic cult of time, with no concern for mundane happenings. Recent work has given reason to believe that some stelae mark events such as the birth or accession of a temporal ruler, and this may show that there were ruling dynasties, although it does not necessarily follow, as has been claimed, that the Maya 'were ruled by secular lords who drew their power from lineage and from conquest'. The facts are not

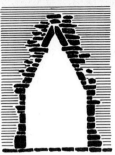

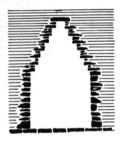

40 Four varieties of corbelled vault, compared with semicircular and pointed arches. The third variety has wooden crossties, which may be compared with the polished black stone ones seen in *Ill. 39*

Ills 37–39

irreconcilable. The most prominent features in a ceremonial centre have a sacred character, which is not invalidated by the discovery of tombs beneath some of the pyramids, and there is no reason why a religious hierarchy should not come to exercise secular control – there are not a few prince-bishops in European history and an episcopal president is still with us – neither is there any reason why a succession should not be established in one clerical family, like the Assyrian patriarchs. The figures carved on stelae were probably rulers, but most are so loaded with insignia as to give the impression that the office mattered more than the man, as might be expected with a sacred ruler.

Ceremonial centres differed greatly in size and importance. At the lowest level were very simple ones, consisting perhaps of a couple of oblong mounds and a small pyramid serving a group of peasant houses. A number of these appear to have been tributary to larger ones, consisting, say, of three courts with at least one imposing pyramid. Several of these in their turn might be subject to a major one like Tikal. There were infinite variations in details, but this seems to have been the general pattern. The

41 Temple of the Sun, Palenque, with remains of elaborately modelled stucco decoration and roof-comb, standing on a low pyramid. Late Classic Maya

centres were all composed of elements of the same kind – platforms and pyramids arranged round courts, ball courts, causeways and so on – but they differed greatly in execution. The towering steep pyramids of Tikal give a very different impression from the much lower ones of Palenque, and the flat tombstone-like stelae of Tikal are far from the rounded, sculptural forms of Copán. Palenque excels in low-relief carving and stucco modelling, and Uxmal is famous for its long, low façades loaded with decoration in stone mosaic.

Ill. 30
Ill. 41

Ill. 36

Maya architecture as a whole was concerned with the grouping of great masses about open spaces, and little interest was taken in interiors. The temples which crowned the great pyramids were small and dark inside, roofed with wooden beams, or corbelled vaults in which each successive horizontal course of stone oversails that below it, until finally the remaining gap can be bridged by a single stone. A roof of either kind was generally crowned with a towering mass of masonry with a carved roof-comb at the top, designed purely for external effect.

Ill. 40

Ill. 41

It has already been suggested that most of the carved hieroglyphic inscriptions which are so notable a feature

42 Page from the Dresden Codex, a manuscript painted on bark-cloth sized with lime and screen-folded. It is thought to have been made *c.* A D 1200, a copy of an older one dating from the Classic period. It shows divinatory almanacs with Maya gods, bar-and-dot numerals, and other glyphs (*see Ills 45, 46*)

Ill. 42

of Maya ceremonial centres were concerned with the passage of time under the appropriate gods, and that some may have recorded events in the life of ruling families, but the same type of writing was painted on strips of bark-cloth sized with lime, and the three surviving books of such strips or pages (codices, as they are called) contain also astronomical matter and divinatory almanacs. Two factors allowed a beginning to be made with their decipherment, namely the survival of several Maya dialects as spoken languages, and the records left by Diego de Landa, third Bishop of Yucatán, in the middle of the sixteenth century. Landa gave us a description of the calendar, and the glyphs, or pictographic symbols, of the days and twenty-day 'months'. He also tried to reduce Maya glyphs to an alphabet, which they are not. His method was to pronounce the letters of the alphabet, in Spanish, and ask his informant, an educated Maya, to write down glyphs denoting those sounds. The result was not at all what he intended and has led to confusions and controversies which are not yet ended, but indirectly it has resulted in the decipherment of certain glyphs (for example he said 'be' – pronounced 'bay' – for 'b', and his informant drew a foot, the Maya glyph for journey or road). On these foundations, archaeologists, linguists, astronomers and others have by laborious study and brilliant deduction built up little by little our present body of knowledge. Much has been read, but the subject is intensely difficult and many glyphs still evade us. Most appear to represent words, a few perhaps syllables of compound words. They even vary in nature – some make use of the combination of sound and sight which we call 'rebus' writing, some are pictorial, and some ideographic.

A centre of the first rank is Copán, which lies in the extreme south-east of the Maya area in the Republic of Honduras. It is in a remote valley where tropical plants flourish but the hills round about are clothed with pines. It was established late, long after Tikal and Uaxactun. In the fifth century AD, some time after the Classic period had begun elsewhere, some members of the Maya hierarchy arrived in the valley, where they found people who had maintained a simpler way of life, similar to that of the earliest villages in the Valley of Mexico. By some means, perhaps a religious conversion, they induced them

Ill. 43

43 Reconstruction by Tatiana Proskouriakoff of the nucleus of the Classic Maya ceremonial centre of Copán, Honduras. Centre and right, the Acropolis; left foreground, the Great Plaza

to provide labour for building the first sanctuaries on the site. Time passed, the cultivation of the valley was intensified, and the great ceremonial centre was gradually formed, as well as a multitude of smaller ones scattered over the valley. Eventually there stood a magnificent group of buildings, now called the Acropolis, which centred in a great platform still covering twelve acres, from which rose a complex mass of pyramids, temples, terraces and courts, towering above the river which later cut much of it away. Even in its ruin, partly rescued from the forest and repaired, it is a breath-taking sight, though it is but a shadow of what, in its glory, it must have been.

To the north of the Acropolis lies a great space enclosed by terraces, forming a series of courts. The northernmost of these, the Great Plaza, is 250 feet square, and is bounded on three sides by tiers of stone steps, which perhaps served as seats, with a pyramid in the midst of the fourth. In and about it stand nine stelae, in this case

Ill. 44

44 Stela B, probable date AD 731. Late Classic Maya. From the Great Plaza, Copán, Honduras

monoliths about twelve feet high, each with a stiff, richly dressed, dignified figure in high relief on the front and hieroglyphic inscriptions recording dates on the sides and in some cases on the back. The figures, each of whom bears a sort of sceptre with a serpent head on either end, supported on his forearms across his chest, are probably rulers of Copán. Each stela has a carved block, perhaps an altar, standing in front of it. The stelae in the Great Plaza range from AD 616 to 782, but the two earliest, dated 616 and 676, must have been put up before the enclosing terraces were built, because the first was re-erected on top of the western terrace and a niche was formed in the eastern terrace to avoid disturbing the second.

The religion to which all this was dedicated doubtless had its origin in some form of nature worship, designed to promote the fertility of the crops, with a few gods such as those of the rain, the wind and the maize, to which was

45, 46 Itzamná, the Maya old god, or god of fire, *above*, and Chac, the Maya long-nosed rain god, carrying a hafted stone axe, *below*. Both from the Dresden Codex, *cf. Ill. 42*

47 Stone lintel from Yaxchilán (formerly called Menché), Chiapas, showing a devotee who is drawing a cord with thorns through his tongue kneeling in front of a priest. The blood falls on bark-paper in a basket, ready to be offered. Probably *c.* AD 750. Late Classic Maya

48 The Ball Court, looking north from a ▷ pyramid on the Acropolis, Copán, with the Great Plaza beyond. Probably late eighth century AD. Beneath the court was another, dated *c.* AD 514, and yet another below. Note the three marker stones on the axis

Ill. 45

early added a god of fire, called Itzamná, the Old God, the head of them all. In Classic times there were in addition thirteen gods of the upper world, nine gods of the underworld, four personages known as *bacabs* who stood at the cardinal points and supported the sky, a god of death, gods of the sun, the moon and Venus, and many others. Days, months and the numbers attached to them all had their patron gods, or were themselves deified. Some gods were benevolent, some the reverse, and some

Ill. 46

gods had more than one aspect; thus Chac, the rain god is sometimes thought of as four Chacs, each associated with a cardinal point and coloured accordingly. The colours were red for east, yellow for south, black for west and white for north, and were constantly associated with these directions, the *bacabs*, for example, being so coloured.

Judging by what was recorded as happening in later times, the ceremonies included prayer, the burning of

incense, dancing, and sacrificial offering, preceded by fasting and continence as a preparation, and ending with feasting. It is certain that men made offerings of their own blood, drawn from tongue, ears and other parts, using aloe thorns, sometimes attached to a string, but human sacrifice was comparatively rare. Doubtless precious things like jade were among the offerings. Great ceremonies were accompanied by orchestras with trumpets, drums and rattles.

Ill. 47

There was also a ceremonial ball-game, and the court where it was played lies just north of the Acropolis. It was apparently built in the eighth century A D, and was the third to be constructed on the site. It is an elongated rectangular space with the floor spread out slightly at the ends like a Roman I, contained on either side by a block of masonry with a sloping top in which are set three stone macaw heads on either side. Behind each of these blocks rises a temple-crowned platform. Set in the floor along

Ill. 48

49 Stone ball-court marker, Chinkultic, Chiapas, showing player with the parts liable to injury armoured, including the right leg, and wearing a plumed headdress, with two blocks and a border of glyphs

Ill. 49

the axis are three weathered stone markers; those from the previous court which are disks bearing elaborately carved armoured figures representing players were found buried underneath in good condition. The game, which involved from one to seven players a side at different times but not more than three among the Classic Maya, was played by propelling a heavy solid rubber ball to and fro, but how the Maya scored at this time is not known, although later courts had vertical sides bearing a stone ring, and any player who put the ball through it won outright. The game was played throughout Middle America, but its origin is lost in antiquity and its meaning and the way it was played may well have varied. It survived until the Spanish Conquest, and Spanish chroniclers say that the ball could be hit with hips, thighs and elbows, but not with the feet. A constant feature of the dress of players is a gauntlet on the right hand, a pad on the right knee, and a shoe on the right foot, but these appear to have been to protect these members from the floor rather than the ball. Apart from these there is a great variety; some are shown naked except for a loin-cloth and the chroniclers say that they suffered severe bruises and sometimes fatal injuries; others, like those on the Copán markers, were

50 Altar Q, in the west court of the Acropolis, Copán. A date on the top is *c.* AD 776. The sides bear sixteen dignitaries seated on glyphs, thought to denote the centres whence they came. It has been suggested that this represents an astronomical congress to determine the correction needed to reconcile the Maya 365-day year with the solar year

well padded and richly adorned. The elaborate nature of the courts and the temples attached to them show that the game had an important function, probably to promote the fertility of the soil. In post-Classic times, when new influences came to the Maya from Central Mexico, it was associated with human sacrifice, and a member of a losing team might have his head cut off by one of the winners. There is no reason to believe that matters were carried to this extreme by the Classic Maya at Copán!

The Maya surpassed all other American peoples in their knowledge of mathematics and astronomy, and in the complexity of their calendar. This could only have been achieved by discipline, self-effacing co-operation between many people over many generations, and a great love of order, and all that we know of the Maya tells us that this is just what their character would lead to. Copán was probably the leading astronomical centre, and its priests knew the length of the solar year to a degree of accuracy slightly greater than the modern or Gregorian Calendar we now use. A carved altar there shows representatives from other centres conferring together possibly to decide on the correction necessary to harmonize the conventional 365-day Maya year with the solar year.

Ill. 50

51 Maya numerals. *Far left*, bar-and-dot number 9 with head glyph of *baktun*. *Left*, zero (or completion) sign with head glyph of *tun*. *Below*, bar-and-dot number 8144, consisting of dot at top (8000), zero units of 400, 7 units of 20, and 4 digits

Ill. 51

Ill. 52

Ill. 52

Their 365-day year consisted of 18 months of 20 numbered days, plus an unlucky 5-day period. They also observed a 260-day ceremonial cycle of 20 named days combined with the numbers 1 to 13. These two cycles ran on in harmony, and a day named in the two cycles did not repeat itself until 52 years later. They also counted each day from an arbitrary beginning far back in time, which we believe to be 3113 BC, and they expressed this in days (*kins*), periods of 20 days (*uinals*), 360 days (*tuns*), 7200 days (*katuns*) and 144,000 days (*baktuns*). Their normal mathematical system was vigesimal (*i.e.* based on a unit of 20), but when dealing with time they substituted a factor of 18 for the normal 20 in forming a *tun*, because it made that unit 360 days, the nearest multiple of 20 to a year. When carving a date they added glyphs connected with the moon, Venus, the appropriate gods of the night and day, and many others.

As has been said, days, months, numbers, *katuns*, and other periods were under the patronage of gods, a point which is emphasized by a rare type of inscription found on one of the stelae in the Great Plaza at Copán, in which the numbers are shown as gods in the guise of Maya bearers at a pause in their journey through time, when they have laid down their burdens the *baktuns*, *katuns*, etc., and in some cases the forehead bands with which they carried them can be seen. As an example, the top-right-hand glyph in this inscription shows the number 9 carrying the *baktun* glyph. Full-figure glyphs of this kind for numbers are rare and those for numbers 1 to 19 are more commonly shown by a head alone.

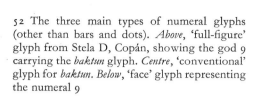

52 The three main types of numeral glyphs (other than bars and dots). *Above*, 'full-figure' glyph from Stela D, Copán, showing the god 9 carrying the *baktun* glyph. *Centre*, 'conventional' glyph for *baktun*. *Below*, 'face' glyph representing the numeral 9

Any day, then, was under the patronage of many gods, some well disposed and some malevolent, and some more powerful than others, and the success of an undertaking would depend on the patrons of the day it began on. It was therefore important to the Maya that the various calendar cycles should be correctly related, and properly synchronized, so that they should know who the patrons of a given day really were. It was also vital to consult a priest who understood the attributes of the gods before starting any important undertaking, and to perform the required ceremonies to propitiate them.

Numbers of any size can be written by columns of bars and dots in a vigesimal system, using dots for units up to 4 and bars for 5 and its multiples up to 15; numbers up to 19 are placed at the bottom, multiples of 20 up to 380 (20×19) above them, followed by multiples of 400, and so on. In a positional system of notation like this it is necessary to have a symbol corresponding to our zero, and the Maya had such a symbol, but they seem to have thought of it as meaning rather completion – a complete number of the appropriate units to make up one of the next higher ones – than nothing.

In A D 800 the last hieroglyphic inscription was carved at Copán. No further building was done and shortly afterwards the hierarchy disappeared. During the century which followed, the same happened at Quiriguá, Piedras Negras, Tikal, Uaxactún and the other southern centres. We do not know why this happened, but the most probable reason is that their religion had grown away from the people, the cult of time was being developed for its own sake, and much of what went on in the sanctuaries did nothing to promote the fertility of the fields. There is also some evidence that disturbances in the Valley of Mexico had their echo here, and that this played its part in setting off changes which were ready to take place. Whatever the reason, the Acropolis of Copán was abandoned to the forest, and the peasants who continued to cultivate the valley only visited it occasionally to burn incense to the Chacs or the maize god, or to bury their dead.

Teotihuacán

Teotihuacán, in the Valley of Mexico some distance from the lake on the north-east side, differed from the Maya centres in, having a dense population round its ceremonial centre and it can therefore be described as a true city. That this was possible must have been due to the use in this open country of a different agricultural system from the slash-and-burn method used by the lowland Maya. It has been suggested that extensive irrigation may have been employed but no positive evidence for it has been found. A possible alternative explanation is that a much-extended scheme of *chinampas*, the misnamed 'floating gardens' which survive at Xochimilco and a few other places near Mexico City, may have existed in favoured places round the lake. The constant addition of floating vegetation and mud dredged from the canals surrounding them to the surface of these garden plots makes them exceedingly fertile, so they could have supported a large population.

Ref. 12

Although Teotihuacán had an extremely widespread influence, not only on the Maya centres but also on those of Oaxaca and the Gulf Coast, it was relatively short-lived. The earliest signs of activity there are about 100 B C, compared with 600 B C at Tikal and 800 B C at Monte Albán; the main building period was between A D 150 and 300, whereas Tikal continued active until after A D 800,

53 The old pyramid in the Ciudadela, Teotihuacán, showing rows of feathered serpents alternating with rain god masks. It was at one time covered by a later pyramid, cf. *Ill. 54*

54 Central pyramid in the Cuidadela, Teotihuacán. Each stage shows the form of slope and panel profile characteristic of Teotihuacán. Different forms are seen at Monte Albán, Tula and other sites. The older pyramid (*Ill. 53*) is behind on the right

and the ceremonial centre was burnt and laid in ruins shortly after AD 600.

Ill. 55

The nucleus of Teotihuacán is a great avenue at least two miles long, running approximately north–south. At the north end is a large terraced pyramid, and there is an even larger one some way to the south on the east side. The avenue is lined with terraced platforms with a highly characteristic profile which is found on all terraced constructions on the site, each step consisting of a heavily framed vertical panel overshadowing a much lower slope. There are numerous groups of buildings on both sides of the road, a few of which have been excavated and restored. Most of them are thought to have been the dwellings of the ruling class, and they consist of courts

55 The avenue which forms the nucleus of Teotihuacán, looking south from the 'Pyramid of the Moon'. Note the slope and panel profile of the terraced platforms. The 'Pyramid of the Sun' is on the left

surrounded by flat-roofed buildings with open fronts composed of an embattled cornice supported by square columns. On the east side there is also a large court, the Ciudadela, surrounded by terraced platforms with a comparatively small pyramid towards its east end, masking an older one, partly excavated, whose panels frame feathered serpents, carved in low relief except for the heads which are in the round and grin outwards from the surface of the pyramid. The serpent heads alternate with grotesque rain-god heads, with the eyes surrounded with rings like a pair of spectacles. Many fragmentary wall-paintings have been found in the ruins, and the rain god is a frequent subject, which shows a preoccupation with water and probably a shortage.

Ill. 54

Ill. 53

Ill. 56

56 *Above*, part of a wall painting at Tetitla, Teotihuacán showing the rain god with an enormous plumed head-dress bearing an owl-like rain god mask. Scrolls representing water and other objects flow from his hands

57, 58 *Left*, a hard stone (diorite) *hacha* showing a male head with dolphin crest from El Tajín, Veracruz. *Opposite*, the main pyramid at El Tajín, Veracruz. The niches, of which there are 365, perhaps representing the days of the year, are characteristic of this area

The Gulf Coast

A civilization of similar character to that of the Classic Maya and Teotihuacán grew up in the lowlands of Veracruz, where the greatest known site is Tajín. Here are found pyramids, platforms, courts and all the usual features of ceremonial centres. The main pyramid has six *Ill. 58* stages decorated with deep square niches which give it a special character, and there are at least six ball courts decorated with reliefs showing scenes of death and human sacrifice. The site continued to flourish through Toltec times until about 1200, and it may be that the custom of human sacrifice by removing the heart was learnt from them, but the possibility that it originated here cannot be dismissed. Some superbly carved objects called *yugos*, *palmas* and *hachas* from this region may be copies in stone *Ill. 57* of protective belts and attachments which were used in the ball-game.

CHAPTER FOUR

The Coming of the Warriors

Little is known of what happened in Central Mexico in the three centuries which followed the destruction of Teotihuacán, although an indication is given by Xochicalco in Morelos to the south of the valley. The main building at this hill-top site is a pyramid bearing carvings which show strong Maya influence, and which is believed to date from Late Classic times, but the place continued in use later and was then fortified. The fortifications here and elsewhere were a response to a new régime of war and violence, accompanied by human sacrifice on a large scale. This was connected with the rise in Central Mexico early in the tenth century of the Toltecs, who were predominantly barbarians from the desert areas to the northwest, though they came to be closely associated in a way which is not fully understood with civilized groups from the east and south-east. They soon acquired much of the civilization of these groups and of the settled inhabitants of the Valley of Mexico, so much so that the later Aztecs looked back on their time as a golden age. The rapidity with which this occurred has given rise to some perplexity, but the way may have been prepared by gradual infiltration and contact during the centuries after the fall of Teotihuacán. The barbarian element are known as the Tolteca-Chichimeca, and they were the first of several

59 Bowl of Mazapan Ware, the most typical Toltec pottery, decorated with groups of wavy lines painted with a multiple brush in orange on buff

waves of Náhuatl-speaking Chichimec peoples to invade Central Mexico.

However much the Toltecs may have owed to their predecessors in the Mexican uplands, they developed well-marked cultural features of their own. They had a characteristic style of sculpture and easily recognized types of pottery, particularly that known to archaeologists as Mazapan Ware, decorated with groups of wavy parallel lines in orange on a buff ground. They were in a sense a cosmopolitan people with widespread contacts, and they received influences and actual imports from several directions. One of their gods, Xipe, the Flayed One, whose priests danced in the flayed skin of a sacrificed slave, typifying the fresh green covering of the earth in spring, seems to have originated in Oaxaca, although he may have been known in Teotihuacán. Imported wares figure among their pottery, notably a lustrous greyish-black to brown ware, called from its appearance Plumbate, which came from the Pacific Coast, and they are credited with the introduction of metal ornaments from as far away as Panama and Colombia.

Ill. 59

Ills 95, 96

Ill. 60

60 Bowl representing a dog, with inlaid shell eyes. Of plumbate, a lustrous ware which in some cases has a true glaze; it is named for its appearance, not for any lead content. It was a widespread trade ware in Toltec times

A few years after the middle of the tenth century, Tula in Hidalgo was founded as the Toltec capital. The founder was a ruler called Topíltzin, who introduced the worship of the feathered serpent, Quetzalcóatl, and took his name. Feathered serpent worship had long been practised at Teotihuacán. Judging by the numerous symbols and representations of Quetzalcóatl there it became very prominent at Tula, where the main pyramid seems to have supported his temple. This pyramid has lost most of its original facing, but part is still faced with stone panels bearing rows of jaguars and coyotes, eagles eating human hearts, and representations of Quetzalcóatl as the morning star. The eagles and jaguars must typify the military orders which later became so important among the Aztecs. On top of the pyramid stand four colossal basalt statues of Toltec warriors and four square columns bearing reliefs of warriors, both of which formerly supported the roof of the temple, and a pair of feathered serpent columns which flanked the doorway. Behind this pyramid is a wall bearing a carved and painted frieze showing serpents eating human bodies almost reduced to skeletons, with a cresting in the form of a series of sections of conch-shells, a symbol of Quetzalcóatl. In the court in front of the pyramid are great colonnades of square columns, the remains of halls one of which covered the approach to the temple stairway.

Ill. 61

Ill. 63

Ill. 62

Ill. 61

After a few years a faction which adhered to the worship of Tezcatlipoca, the tribal god of the Tolteca-Chichimeca, whose name means Smoking Mirror in Náhuatl from the obsidian mirror which replaced his right foot, expelled Topíltzin Quetzalcóatl and his followers. After various vicissitudes they came to the Gulf Coast and sailed away, and one legend in which Topíltzin promised to return and claim his own had its consequences many years later when Moctezuma thought that Cortés and his followers were they.

61–63 The North pyramid, *above*, sometimes called the Temple of Quetzalcóatl, at Tula, showing colonnades, the remains of halls at the base of the stairway, and tenons which secured the original facing. On the top are four giant figures representing Toltec warriors, behind them is a row of square columns with warriors carved in low relief, and in front is a pair of feathered serpent columns at the top of the stair; these supported the temple roof. *Left*, one of the warriors and two of the columns seen *above*. Each is built up of four sections of basalt tenoned together. Details of the warriors' dress and equipment are meticulously shown. They are thought to be incarnations of the Morning Star, an aspect of Quetzalcóatl. *Opposite*, a detail of the remains of the facing on the north side of the pyramid, showing bands of jaguars and coyotes, alternating with bands of birds eating human hearts and monsters symbolizing Quetzalcóatl as the Morning Star

The Toltec domination lasted little more than two centuries. They took the sword and they perished by it. Tula was overthrown and destroyed about 1170 by a new wave of Náhuatl-speaking invaders also called Chichimeca. The downfall of the Toltecs ushered in a period of chaos, the history of which is complex and not altogether clear. Its decipherment does not depend entirely upon archaeology, since the period is covered by a series of records, some written before the Spanish Conquest in the native picture writing, and others embodying native oral traditions, written in Náhuatl or Spanish in European characters shortly after the Conquest. These manuscripts or codices were painted on bark paper with a surface dressing of lime, and took the form of 'rebus' writing of a sort: thus the Aztec capital, Tenochtitlán, was represented by a cactus (*nochtli*) sprouting from a stone (*tena*). This recalls their legend that the site was indicated to them by a white eagle representing the god

64, 65 Chac-Mools, reclining stone figures carrying a bowl on the stomach, probably for offerings. They are characteristic of the Toltec period. The one *above* is from Tula and the one *left* from the Temple of the Warriors, Chichén Itzá, Yucatán

66, 67 Temple of the Warriors, Chichén Itzá, Yucatán. Toltec Maya period. The entrance, *below*, is flanked by a pair of feathered serpent columns symbolizing Quetzalcóatl, which supported the lintel on their rattlesnake tails. The roof was supported by square columns with low-relief warriors like those at Tula (*Ill. 62*). The trunk-like objects on the walls belong to Maya long-nosed rain gods, illustrating the fusion of Maya and Toltec cultures

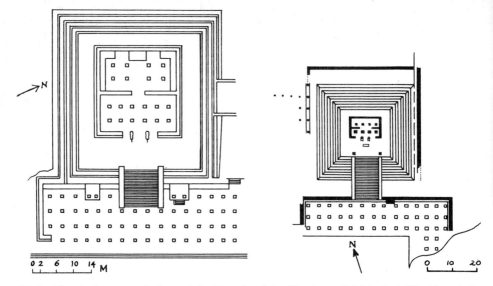

68, 69 The similar ground-plans of the Temple of the Warriors, Chichén Itzá (*Ill. 66*) and the North pyramid at Tula (*Ill. 61*) compared. Each has a small two-roomed temple on top of the pyramid approached by a steep flight of steps, and columns in front

Huitzilopochtli, who perched on a cactus growing from a stone on an island in the Lake of Texcoco. The records are often obscure or contradictory, so the reconstruction of the story is far from easy.

Ill. 73

Events in Central Mexico had their echo far away in Yucatán. The great Maya centre of Chichén Itzá was abandoned for a time, beginning about A D 900, but it was reoccupied and transformed towards the end of the century. Some of the older buildings were refurbished and many new ones built, including two great temple-crowned pyramids, an imposing ball court, and a number of platforms veneered with carved stones. The Temple of the Warriors, one of the main temples, has a pair of feathered rattlesnake columns at the entrance, the roof was supported by square columns bearing warriors carved in low relief, the pyramid has carved reliefs showing eagles, jaguars and other beasts holding hearts, and below it are great colonnades. The beasts and birds appear also

Ill. 71

Ill. 66
Ill. 67

70 Platform showing rows of human skulls impaled on poles, Chichén Itzá. It was probably the base of the *tzompantli*, a rack on which the skulls of sacrificed victims were placed at Toltec and later sites

on one of the platforms, and another bears rows of skulls impaled on poles. Wall-paintings show two different peoples in conflict, and a carved frieze in the ball court shows their teams lined up facing one another across a large ball bearing a skull, the foremost player of one team holding the head of his opposite number which he has cut off with a stone knife. From the victim's neck sprout serpents surrounding a great plant, doubtless fertilized by his blood. These features recall both the ideology and the architecture of Tula, and the carvings of warriors and predatory birds and beasts are so similar as to point to a direct connexion. Maya traditions speak of the arrival from the west of a great lord named Kukulcán, meaning Feathered Serpent in their tongue, in the *katun* which ended in 987, when a new people, the Itzá, also arrived, and Kukulcán was probably their leader. The coincidence is too great for there to be any serious doubt that Kukulcán and the Itzá were the Toltec Quetzalcóatl and

Ill. 70

Ills 68, 69

his followers who had been expelled from Tula not long before. Their opponents in the carved and painted scenes are identified in various ways with the Maya, and traditions which survived into Spanish times show their feeling towards the Itzá, who lacked, they said, sound judgment, orderliness and wisdom, besides introducing lewdness which led to sickness and disaster. Chichén Itzá was a particularly sacred site, since it had a very large well or *cenote*, really a pool about 200 feet across surrounded by cliffs some 65 feet high, which was a centre of pilgrimage to which people came from far to sacrifice objects and human beings by throwing them in. It is connected by a causeway with the second great temple, said to be that of Kukulcán. The cult was active in Toltec-Maya times, and it survived the fall of Chichén Itzá and continued until the Spaniards stopped it.

Ill. 75

Ill. 74

Ill. 72

At some other Maya centres in Yucatán, such as Uxmal, Toltec influence left few traces, and these seem to have appeared without an intermediate period of abandonment.

Chichén Itzá was the most important place in Yucatán from the coming of the Itzá until about 1200, when it gave place to Mayapan. This was an ill-planned walled city, whence another group of Itzá established a centralized rule over most of Yucatán. Built in an infertile, rocky place, it must have derived its sustenance more from tribute than from farming. Its religious buildings are a

72 The Castillo, or Temple of Kukulcán, Chichén Itzá, seen from the Temple of the Warriors. Within the pyramid is a slightly earlier and smaller one, still surmounted by its temple. This has been revealed by tunnelling. It was found to contain a red-painted stone throne in the form of a jaguar, with inlaid 'spots' of jade and jade eyes

71 The great Ball Court at Chichén Itzá. It is of characteristic Toltec type, with vertical walls and stone rings. The benches at the bottom bear reliefs on their sloping faces showing opposing Maya and Toltec teams, with the leader of the losing one having had his head cut off by the leader of the winning one

83

73-75 *Above*, reconstruction of Chichén Itzá by Tatiana Proskouriakoff, looking from near the sacred *cenote* along the causeway to the Castillo, with the Temple of the Warriors on the left and the great Ball Court on the right. Beyond are the older Classic Maya buildings. *Left*, a thin gold disk, one of many dredged from the sacred *cenote*. These were probably imported readymade from Panama, and decorated on the spot by embossing. It shows a Maya prisoner being sacrificed by a Toltec chief by cutting out the heart. *Opposite*, the sacred *cenote* of Chichén Itzá. Yucatán is limestone country, and all the water is found below the surface in pools and wells produced by solution

pale reflection of those at Chichén Itzá, inferior both in size and in construction, and a lack of jade and fine pottery shows a general deterioration in the arts. Mayapán in its turn fell to a rival group about 1450 and was sacked. There was nothing to succeed it except a group of small independent states, constantly at war with one another, which the Spaniards found when they arrived in the succeeding century. They have left no buildings or significant archaeological remains, but there was one remarkable survival. The Itzá who were driven out of Chichén Itzá in about 1200 fled to Tayasal, on an island in Lake Petén far to the south. Here they kept up their old customs right through the times of the Spanish Conquest and beyond it, and retained their independence until 1697.

Ills 83, 84
 In and around north-west Oaxaca lived the Mixtecs. Little is known about their origins, but their pictorial manuscripts have enabled Professor Alfonso Caso to trace the genealogies of their rulers back to before A D 700. In the thirteenth century there are signs that they began to push into the Valley of Oaxaca, and the process seems to have been intensified in the fifteenth century. The result was the development of a new type of architecture, owing it is true a good deal to Zapotec traditions but with new features, particularly elaborate relief panels of stone mosaic composed of angular geometrical forms such as the step fret. The best examples are on the well-known

Ills 76, 77 buildings at Mitla, but they are also found on the façades of stone-lined tombs at Yagul. Zapotec tombs were some-

Ill. 82 times reused, as in the case of the famous Tomb 7 at Monte Albán, where there was a wealth of gold jewellery and other treasures. Besides these elaborate gold ornaments, made by the cire-perdue process or by hammering

Ills 78–81 sheet gold, they brought their own pottery styles, delicately carved bones, turquoise mosaics, ornaments of rock-crystal and vessels of *tecali* (Mexican onyx, a form

Ill. 78 of travertine). Their polychrome pottery is particularly

76, 77 Façade of the Group of the Columns, Mitla, Oaxaca, the main external feature of one of several courts built under Mixtec direction or influence. *Below*, a room in the Group of the Columns. The stone mosaics are characteristic of these Mixtec/Zapotec buildings. The rooms formerly had flat timber roofs and were very dark; some of them were still occupied at the time of the Spanish Conquest

78, 79 Mixtec tripod bowls from Oaxaca. *Left*, of lustrous ware, painted in orange, white, black and maroon, and *right*, white

notable. These, together with their painted screenfold deerskin manuscripts, which include most of the finest surviving Mesoamerican examples, exemplify the Mixteca-Puebla art style, which had a profound effect on Aztec art.

The Aztecs

The fall of Tula and the arrival of various groups of Chichimeca resulted in the establishment of a number of small states, some of them civilized Toltec survivals and some ruled by the newcomers. These are generally believed to have been savage nomads and many of them doubtless were, but the rapidity with which they adopted the settled agricultural pattern of life and much of the civilization of the Toltecs suggests that some at least of them were farmers driven in from the marginal lands to the north-west by a dry climatic cycle. The latest and most barbarous group to arrive were the Tenochcas, generally called the Aztecs, and after various reverses

80, 81 Cup and bowl of Cholula Ware. Mixtec pottery from Puebla, of a type frequently taken to Tenochtitlán as tribute

which they richly deserved they settled on some un-occupied islands in the swamps by the lake and founded their twin capitals Tenochtitlán and Tlatelolco in the first half of the fourteenth century (1325 or possibly 1345).

Between this time and the latter part of the fifteenth century they transformed themselves. They became mercenaries and then allies of the Tepanecs of Azcapotzalco, from whom they learnt a great deal, and in 1428 they overthrew them and emerged as the predominant tribe in the valley. In little more than a century they developed from a tribe divided into clans, knowing no authority but that of their chiefs, into an organized state under an absolute monarch supported by an hereditary aristocracy. It was at the same time what Caso has described as a military theocracy, the king was also a priest and all the high functionaries of the state had been educated in the priestly schools. The monarch was elected from among the royal family by a council of the highest nobles, priests

82 Mixtec gold pendant, Tomb 7, Monte Albán, showing, from above, ball game, sun disk, moon glyph, and earth symbol

83, 84 Pages from the Mixtec Codex Nuttall illustrating the story of Lady Three Flint. *Above*, she gives birth to a child, right, then dives into a hole in the mountainside leading to a purifying bath, bottom left. *Below*, she is seen offering sacrifices after the delivery of her child and then sitting with her husband Lord Five Flower, above, in the palace

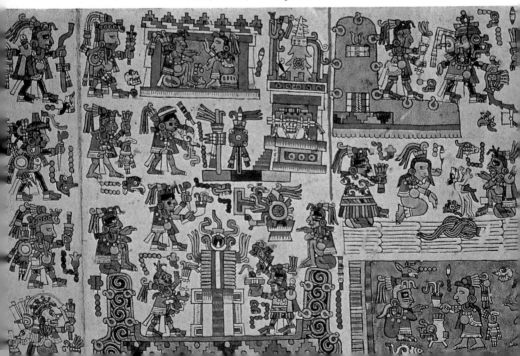

85 The surviving part of the double stairway leading to the twin temples on the great *teocalli* at Tlatelolco, the subsidiary ceremonial centre of Tenochtitlán. Several superimposed pyramids have been found in the excavation, besides smaller structures. Bernal Diaz records Cortés' ascent of the pyramid with Moctezuma

and warriors, which also chose the four great lords of the realm. Two of these were members of the royal family, and one of them was later elected to be the next sovereign. There was also a sort of Grand Vizier, the Cihuacóatl (meaning 'snake-woman'), who acted for the king in his absence. It is true that the clans (*calpulli*) survived as land-holding corporations, but class divisions developed between and within them, and one included the royal family. The system showed signs of obsolescence by the sixteenth century, and some important categories, the merchants, warriors and serfs, were outside the clans. Society was, indeed, highly specialized. There were the three warrior orders of Eagles, Tigers and Arrows, who held a position of special honour; priests of many grades; a privileged class of merchants who travelled abroad with something approaching diplomatic privileges, and crafts-

Ills 88–90

86, 87 Sculpture showing feathered serpent typifying Quetzalcóatl, *above*, and *left*, Quetzalcóatl in the guise of Ehecatl, the wind god, wearing his long-nosed mask, and Tlaloc, the rain god. Both from Codex Magliabecchi

men of many types. There was an increasing emphasis on militarism, and this was bound up with religion, in which the old pantheon, the gods of agriculture and rain, with Quetzalcóatl, Xipe and the rest, had acquired new aspects, and had been joined by the special gods of the Chichimeca. The patron of the Aztecs was Huitzilopochtli, the sun god, a young warrior who was born anew every morning of Coatlicué, the ghastly old earth goddess with the skirt of serpents. His elder sister and brothers, the moon and the stars, were provoked to furious jealousy, and each morning he had to overcome them before starting his journey through the sky, borne on a litter as far as the zenith by warriors killed in battle or sacrificed, and thence to the end of the day by women who had died in childbirth. At sunset he was gathered again to the earth. The divine struggle was repeated daily, and the sun had to be strong to repulse the multitude of stars with his fiery serpents, the rays or arrows of light, or the world would come

88–90 Objects referring to the knightly orders. *Above*, stone head of an Eagle Knight, wearing an eagle helmet. *Left*, Aztec war drum (*huehuetl*) from Malinalco, State of Mexico, superbly carved with eagles and jaguars denoting the knightly orders, the sign '4 Earthquake' denoting the age in world history (p. 94), and the sun as an eagle. The whole has been held to symbolize the Wars of Flowers. *Right*, ceremonial *atl atl* or spear-thrower (cf. *Ill. 1*) with gold sheathing showing an Eagle Knight in relief. It is a local type in which the fingers pass through the stone loops. The butt of the spear rests in a groove on the reverse side at the lower end

91, 92 Stone-bladed sacrificial knife, probably Mixtec workmanship, with wooden handle inlaid with turquoise, shell and lignite, representing a crouching Eagle Knight. It was used for human heart sacrifices, such as that shown *left* on a Toltec Maya wall painting at Chichén Itzá (cf. *Ill. 74*)

Ills 91, 92
Ills 93, 94

to an end as it had four times before, and indeed was doomed to do again on a day called '4 Earthquake'.

In the meantime man had to feed the sun with the food of the gods, the *chalchíuatl* or precious fluid, human blood. The Aztecs were the People of the Sun, so it was their special duty and privilege to get prisoners, and to offer him their blood and their hearts. His thirst came to be shared by other gods, hence the notorious ghastly succession of human sacrifices, most of which were performed by cutting out the heart of the victim stretched on a stone before the temple of the god, at the top of its *teocalli* or pyramid. It is said that twenty thousand prisoners were slaughtered at the dedication of the last enlargement of the Great Teocalli in Tenochtitlán. The higher the degree of the victim, the more valuable he was for the purpose,

93, 94 Aztec pottery flute of type played by some victims on their way up the *teocalli* to be sacrificed and a pottery representation of an Aztec god seated on his *teocalli*

and ceremonial conflicts called Wars of Flowers were arranged between the cream of the warriors of different Chichimec tribes to obtain prisoners for sacrifice and to carry the sun through his daily war. Death in battle or on the sacrificial stone was the highest destiny of a warrior, and led him to the highest heaven.

Religion was still bound up with the calendar, and the Aztecs, together with other Mesoamerican peoples, shared the 365-day year and the 260-day cycle or *tonalpohualli*, which have been mentioned in connexion with the Maya. These formed a 52-year cycle, but the Aztecs did not know the higher elaborations of the Maya Calendar. The ending of the cycle, which was always on a day called 1 *Malinalli* (Grass) in the *tonalpohualli*, was a critical time, since it was feared that it might mark the end of the world, and great precautions were taken. Fires were let out, pottery was broken, pregnant women were shut up in granaries lest they turned into wild animals, and children were kept awake lest they turned into rats. A solemn procession of priests marched up the Hill of the Star near Culhuacán, and waited for a certain star called Yohualtecuhtli, perhaps Aldebaran, to pass the zenith and show that the world would continue. A victim was then sacrificed and fire kindled with a drill on a wooden hearth placed in the gash whence his heart had been removed, to be carried to hearths throughout the land. These cycles have archaeological importance, since they were marked by the reconstruction of temple-pyramids, like that of Tenayuca, which was enlarged five times, after the cycles which ended in 1299, 1351, 1403, 1455 and 1507.

During the reigns of Izcóatl, the ruler who overthrew the Tepanecs, and his two successors, Moctezuma I and Axayácatl, the Cihuacóatl was Moctezuma's brother Tlacaélel, a remarkable man who reorganized the state, and, having burnt the books of conquered peoples which might have contradicted him, rewrote Aztec history. He inspired them with the fiction of a glorious past, and the hope of a glorious future in fulfilling their destiny as the People of the Sun. To the fanaticism thus stimulated may be ascribed much of their success in warfare and conquest. Izcóatl consolidated the Aztec position, and in Moctezuma's reign their conquests carried them to Oaxaca and the Gulf Coast, whilst at home Tenochtitlán was rebuilt in stone and beautified. Subsequent rulers subjugated the twin state of Tlatelolco and extended their conquests to the frontier of modern Guatemala; the importance of this is illustrated by an estimate that out of eighty thousand inhabitants of Tenochtitlán and its immediate neighbourhood fifty thousand were sustained by tribute. The monarchy became more and more absolute, and by the time that Moctezuma II was elected in 1502 he was

95, 96 Back and front of an Aztec basalt mask showing the flayed skin from the face of a victim sacrificed to the god Xipe, as worn by his priests. The reverse bears a carving of a priest or the god himself in a flayed skin

regarded as a demigod. His reign was marked by many rebellions of conquered tribes, but he took little part in quelling them, and gave himself largely to the religious aspect of his office. He was profoundly versed in the traditional legends, and the messages he received about the landing of Cortés convinced him that Quetzalcóatl had returned as he had prophesied. The only way to stop him was to invoke other gods, and when this failed to receive him with a good grace. It was useless to fight.

Ills 97, 98

Much of Aztec art reflects the brutality of their religion, and this is seen particularly in much of their stone-carving. Grim-featured gods, Xipe-masks, skulls and serpents all emphasize its grisly character. It was deeply affected by the Mixteca-Puebla style, and many of the objects which are generally regarded as Aztec were made by Mixtec workmen. These include the famous mosaic objects of turquoise, red and white shell, black lignite and brassy pyrite, such as the sacrificial knife handle and the mask made from a human skull in the British Museum. Some stone carvings, among them the great stone of the Emperor Tizoc, which was found near the centre of

Ills 95, 96

Ill. 91

Ill. 99

Ill. 100

97, 98 Examples of Aztec featherwork. *Above*, a head-dress over four feet high, mainly of green quetzal feathers and gold, with some blue, crimson, brown and white feathers, given by Moctezuma to Cortés as a gift to his sovereign. *Left*, an Aztec featherwork shield, showing a blue and purple coyote outlined with gold thread on a pink field, said to be the device of King Ahuitzotl, AD 1486–1502, Moctezuma II's predecessor

99 Front of a human skull, encrusted with a mosaic of turquoise, black lignite, and white shell, with eyes of brassy pyrites, possibly representing the god Tezcatlipoca. Probably Mixtec work

100 Stone commemorating the victories of the Aztec King Tizoc, AD 1481–86, showing him as a god seizing captives shown beneath the glyphs of conquered places. The carving is influenced by the Mixtec manuscript style (cf. *Ills 83, 84*). From the ceremonial centre of Tenochtitlan

Ill. 101

Mexico City, are carved in the style of the Mixtec manuscripts. Much polychrome Mixtec pottery came to Tenochtitlán as tribute, but there were also local pottery styles in graceful shapes with delicate designs in black on orange or red.

It would be natural to believe that the condition of the Aztec nation bore within it the seeds of disaster, that the continual wars and human sacrifices were too great a burden to bear, and that the common people would sooner or later rise against the rulers and the priests. However this may be, the point had not been reached when the Spaniards put an end to it all, although other tribes, like the Tlaxcalans, were only too ready to revolt and to join the newcomers against their oppressors. As the People of the Sun the Aztecs were all part of the

101 Aztec pottery. Left, a grey/black on orange tripod bowl; Aztec III, fifteenth century. Top right, jug, black on dark red; Aztec IV, sixteenth century. Bottom right, a grey/black on orange tripod bowl with a hollow at one end for liquid; Aztec III, fifteenth century

system, and they took it very much for granted. Every able-bodied man was trained to fight, and he could gain honour and advancement by distinguishing himself in battle and by taking prisoners, and in so doing he participated in the sacrifices.

Western Mexico

This area, especially the States of Colima, Jalisco and Nayarit, was generally out of touch with the main centres, and the temple-pyramids and the gods of the high cultures are lacking. The archaeological sequence is very imperfectly known. The area is known mainly for large hollow pottery figures showing human figures, some of them grouped in scenes of daily life, and lively fat dogs. There are also smaller solid figurines, houses and scenes, including

Ill. 103
Ill. 102

102, 103 Colima, West Mexico, is noted for its hollow, pottery figures. *Left*, a pair of 'dancing dogs' of red pottery, partly smudged black dating from the first two centuries A D, and *right*, the figure of a man blowing a conch-shell trumpet

the ball-game. They are much sought by collectors, and most have been looted from deep shaft graves containing multiple burials in side chambers. This is a feature which is found also in Central America and especially in northern South America, areas on much the same cultural level. Recent work has shown that this type of burial had developed by the early centuries A D, and that it had disappeared before the end of the first millennium, when there was a short-lived wave of influence from Central Mexico.

CHAPTER FIVE

The Intermediate Area

The Intermediate Area between Mesoamerica and the Central Andes (Peru and highland Bolivia) never reached the heights of its illustrious neighbours, and was at much the same cultural level as the less developed parts of western Mexico. It received influences from both regions of higher civilization, including maize agriculture from Mexico, metal working from Peru, and a priest-temple-idol complex possibly from both. It has many achievements to its credit, especially in metal working and pottery, but there was little attempt at monumental architecture at any time, and it lacked the hieroglyphic and pictographic writing of Mesoamerica and the political organization of Peru. Government consisted generally of small chiefdoms, although there is evidence from sixteenth-century records as well as from archaeology that federations of small units under a powerful chief were sometimes formed, especially in Ecuador and Colombia. The pattern of chiefdoms of limited territorial extent has resulted in great diversity of art styles, seen best in pottery form and decoration. Our appreciation of the cultural achievements of the area is much limited by bad conditions of preservation, so that perishables seldom survive, in marked contrast to the dry coast of Peru, where the finest textiles may be preserved in mint condition.

Ref. 13

The area has been very unevenly studied and some parts are virtually unknown. It is only recently that attempts at syntheses have been made for parts of it, and these are bounded by modern frontiers rather than natural features, but even they vary so widely within themselves that it is difficult to treat them as units. Outline chronological frameworks exist for some parts, but dating in general is not sufficiently precise to allow correlations over wide areas. This means that the area cannot well be discussed as a whole, but before treating individual parts, an attempt will be made to point out when some significant stages were reached in places where their dates are approximately known.

Ref. 14

Apart from the few traces of early man before about 5000 BC which have already been mentioned, the earliest remains so far discovered are at Cerro Mangote in Panama shortly after that date, where semi-permanent settlements by people who lived by hunting and collecting shell-fish, and used rough pebble tools, have been found. The same way of life continued there for a long time and is still found, accompanied by the first pottery known in Central America, shortly before 2000 BC at Monagrillo, also in Panama. This pottery is of a simple type with incised decoration and a little red painting.

Ill. 104

Pottery appeared much earlier elsewhere. At Puerto Hormiga, on the north coast of Colombia, crude fibre-tempered bowls and rather finer sand-tempered ones date from about 3000 BC, long before any trace of agriculture. At Valdivia and other sites on the Ecuadorian coast, well-made pottery, rarely red-slipped but otherwise decorated only by a variety of incising and stamping techniques, appeared at about the same time. (At neither of these sites are the radiocarbon dates sufficient to indicate which has the priority.) In the case of Puerto Hormiga permanent or semi-permanent settlement was made possible by abundant natural resources – molluscs, fish, small game, nuts,

104 Tetrapod bowl of red-slipped pottery with incised decoration. Lower Valdivia phase, 3000–2300 BC, coast of Ecuador

seeds and roots. At Valdivia, the people were chiefly fishermen, who have left shell fish-hooks and net sinkers, but they also hunted deer. Analogy with Peru suggests that they may have cultivated beans and other plants, but this is by no means certain, and the lack of pottery there for more than a millennium later argues against any contacts. Resemblances between Valdivia pottery and that of Middle Jomon have led to the suggestion that it was introduced from Japan by a boatload of fishermen carried away by a hurricane and drifted across the Pacific by the currents. This implies the pre-existence on the coast of Ecuador of a receptive pre-ceramic fishing community for which evidence has not yet been found and would be difficult to find. Several pre-ceramic complexes of stone implements have recently been reported by E. P. Lanning from the Santa Elena Peninsula, but they all appear to be separated from Valdivia by a long time interval. *Ref. 15*

The introduction of agriculture and the times when it became the predominant means of subsistence in different parts of the area have not been very satisfactorily determined, and this is complicated by the presence of two basic types of agricultural development there. The seed crop, maize, spread from Mesoamerica, presumably in a developed condition, over much of the area, and manioc,

a South American lowland root crop, was the staple in eastern Venezuela, where some believe that it was domesticated. Manioc exists in two varieties, a sweet form which can be eaten without precautions, and a bitter form which needs special treatment to eliminate prussic acid but has the advantage that it can be stored for a limited time. It is assumed that the sweet variety was eaten before the poisonous one, but it leaves no evidence of its presence on archaeological sites, whereas the poisonous one can sometimes be detected by the presence of thick pottery slabs which were used as griddles for roasting cakes made of the flour. These suggest that it was used in western Venezuela, soon after 2000 B C, but they are not numerous enough to indicate a main dependence on the plant until about 1000 B C in northern Colombia and probably western Venezuela. The presence of maize in this area has to be deduced from stone grinding-slabs and hand stones, which indicate that it may have arrived from

Ill. 105

◁ 105 Stone *metate*, or slab on which to grind maize, in the form of a jaguar. Veraguas Province, Panamá, or eastern Costa Rica

106 Polychrome bottle, Province of Coclé, Panamá

Mesoamerica about 700 B C, after which it spread rapidly, but it never displaced manioc from eastern Venezuela. It would be expected earlier in Central America, but no evidence has been reported. It is believed that there were permanent villages there by 300 B C, but, given the much earlier dates at which they are found elsewhere, this is probably too late an estimate for their beginning. The spread of maize from Mesoamerica to Ecuador has been inferred from the establishment of inland villages in well-watered areas to have taken place about 1500 B C, although more direct evidence in the shape of grinding stones is forthcoming from 500 B C onwards.

Central America

The earliest villages show no signs of classes or of an elaborate religious cult. After about A D 300 class differences begin to appear, and are shown by the burial of important people in mounds. A simple type of pottery in

107 Grey anthropomorphic pottery vessel with nose-plaque and 'bandolier' ornaments. Chibcha, Colombia

108, 109 Two stone grotesques. *Right*, ▷ an over lifesize statue of a man with feline fangs, and a trophy head hanging round his neck from San Agustín, Colombia. *Far right*, a stone figure in the form of a celt-shaped slab. South-east Costa Rica

two colours outlined by incision is sufficiently common for this to be called the Zoned Bichrome Stage, but some three-colour and polychrome wares appear towards AD 500. The next three centuries show striking technical developments, with the introduction of gold, jade and other semi-precious stones, and cemeteries where slaves were buried with their masters show further growth of classes. After AD 800 there was a marked increase in population, abundant metal work, stone statues and other carvings, and very diverse pottery styles, including fine polychromes in Costa Rica and especially in Coclé Province, Panama. Planned ceremonial sites with earth mounds arranged round courts are found in Costa Rica, and alignments of stone statues and columns in Panama. Important graves are very richly furnished.

Ref. 16

Ill. 109

Ill. 106

Colombia

It is thought that the highlands were very sparsely populated until the introduction of maize, which encouraged rapid settlement. Specially Colombian features are deep shaft graves with side chambers, and several accomplished local styles in gold and gold-copper alloys with emphasis on cire-perdue casting. Polychrome pottery is rare, but black negative painting over red or red and white is very common, especially in the Cauca Valley, and there is a good deal of figure modelling in monochrome wares, especially in the Chibcha area. Some vessels with two containers, or with two spouts connected by a bridge, recall the Peruvian coast in a general way.

   A noted area is San Augustín in the southern highlands. It is distinguished for its fierce-looking stone statues and

Ills 112, 113

Ill. 107

Ill. 110

Ill. 108

110 Monochrome double vessel with bridge handle. Chibcha, Colombia

its dolmen-like temples covered by mounds, and there is a river-bed on which have been carved figures of men and animals. Dates between the sixth century BC and the twelfth century AD have been obtained there, but the chronology within these limits is obscure.

At the time of the Conquest there were federations, the Chibcha in the highlands round Bogotá and the Tairona in the Sierra Nevada de Santa Marta. The evidence for the Chibcha one is more documentary than archaeological, and there are no signs of substantial structures or of deep middens. It was a Chibcha chief, El Dorado, who on his accession was coated with gold dust, which he offered to the spirit which lived in Lake Guatavita by diving in. The Tairona have left substantial stone terraces, stairways and foundations, but their actual houses and temples were of wood. Sixteenth-century records suggest that their religion had a Mesoamerican character.

Ecuador

The Ecuadorian coast has been more extensively studied than the highlands, and this discussion will be confined to it. The Valdivia fishing villages continued for about two thousand years, a remarkable record of stability, or perhaps stagnation, with few changes except gradual ones in the form and decoration of their monochrome pottery. The main innovation was the appearance, about 2300 BC, of abundant female pottery figurines with elaborate hairstyles. They originated some eight hundred years before their Mesoamerican counterparts, and differ from them

112, 113 *Above*, a gourd-shaped gold vase, about four inches high, between a female figure and an object of uncertain use, both of gold-copper alloy, *tumbaga*. Quimbaya, Cauca Valley, Colombia. *Right*, gold figurine, flat plate, with wire-like details, all cast by the cire-perdue process. Chibcha, Bogotá area, Colombia

in style. The appearance about 2000 BC of new forms of pottery, including stirrup-spouted jars, later so common on the Peruvian coast, and bowls with simple designs in red paint, has been held to mark the arrival of new people, who settled, like their predecessors, exclusively near the sea but on new sites. An odd feature is that these people seem to have lived alongside one another and traded with one another for about one thousand years, and yet each seems to have continued its own ceramic tradition.

About 1500 BC began the settlements in the Guayas Basin, inland but still on the coastal plain, which are

114, 115 Pottery of the Bahía phase, Province of Manabí, Ecuador. *Left*, a hollow, seated figurine. *Above*, a head-rest with reclining figure on base, perhaps showing Asiatic contact, *c*. 200 BC

thought to indicate the coming of maize cultivation from Mesoamerica, and the connexion with that area is supported by a number of features, chiefly in pottery decoration, which are shared with coastal Guatemala, and also by 'napkin-ring' ear-spools of fine polished pottery, which are characteristic of Central Mexico. By about 500 BC a number of distinct cultural provinces had developed on the Ecuadorian coast, most of them reaching an artistic climax each in its own area. One example, the Bahía phase in Manabí Province, has ceremonial structures consisting of low rectangular stone-faced platforms with a stairway at one end, fine polychrome pottery, and an abundance of elaborate mould-made figurines and some pottery stamps for body painting, both of which may point to continuing contacts by sea with Mesoamerica. Different varieties of figurine occur in different provinces, and the elaborate dress of many of them suggests specialized functions and a stratified society. The brief appearance of pottery head-rests, vessels in the form of high-gabled houses with sagging ridge-poles, and certain figurine types has provoked the suggestion that a ship brought them from Asia about 200 BC. After about AD 500 there was a tendency for the local cultural varieties to be merged into larger units, which may reflect the existence of confederations, but they are not easily reconciled with tribal boundaries mentioned in sixteenth-century records. It was a time of increasing population and social differentiation, and there were some towns of considerable size. Pottery diminished in artistic merit and a great deal of it was dull buff or grey, but metal working increased in skill and quantity, both as jewellery and as useful objects. The coast near Manta is known for its stone working – figures, carved slabs and literally hundreds of U-shaped chairs supported by crouching figures of men or animals. Inland, in the Guayas Basin, are many urn burials in mounds, belonging to people of many degrees of importance. A few must have been great chiefs; they are in 'chimneys' consisting of piles of large urns with the bottoms knocked out, and they contain diadems, collars, rings, bowls and other objects of silver and gold in abundance, besides quantities of copper which have enabled the preservation of perishables, including textiles which have shown us that these Ecuadorians shared the weaving skill of the Peruvians. One exceptionally rich burial even had the latest novelty, Venetian glass beads, as well as its aboriginal finery, showing that the Spaniards were not far off and that the story was coming to an end.

The Incas conquered the whole of the highlands after a bitter struggle, but they barely touched the coast. The story of their encounter with the inhabitants of the island of Puná, who drowned their garrison in the troubled waters of the Guayas Estuary, is a matter of history.

116 Chimney burial, one of many found in a large mound on the Babahoyo river, Guayas Basin, lowland Ecuador. Late period, shortly before the Spanish Conquest. The burial, of disarticulated bones, is in the lowest urn

117 Jar showing naked prisoner attacked by an unusually naturalistic jaguar. At this stage, the jaguar cult is generally expressed by human figures with jaguar faces, or merely fangs. Mochica, North coast of Peru, *c.* AD 500

118 Lay figure dressed in richly embroidered mantle and under-garments, specially made for burial with an important man. Paracas, south coast of Peru, *c.* first century AD

119 Peruvian pottery of about the mid-first millennium AD on a piece of ancient Peruvian dark blue gauze. Left, Mochica stirrup-spouted jar representing a dead dignitary. Right, Recuay, North Highlands. The negative black painting shows an animal with a scroll-like crest. The wide flange and lateral spout are also typical. Bottom, spout-and-bridge jar with stylized modelling, painted in many colours. Late Nasca, South Coast

115

CHAPTER SIX

The Growth of Empire

Peru and the Incas

Ill. 120

The Inca Empire had the most elaborate integrated plan of government in ancient America, but it did not arise until the last century of a long story, which has already been traced from its remote beginnings up to the building of the earliest temples in the second millennium B C. It can not be appreciated without some idea of what happened in the intervening period, and of its natural surroundings which are among the most remarkable in the world. The countries which lie along the Andes are lands of contrasts, which are nowhere more marked than in Peru. The great mountain chain with its snow-capped peaks, bleak plateaux and passes, sheltered valleys and deep gorges, forms the backbone of the country, and this is the region from which the Incas came. It falls steeply on either flank, eastwards to the dense forests of the Amazon Basin, and westwards to the narrow, arid coastal plain, crossed by valleys which cradled many of the ancient cultures. The valleys are separated from one another by miles of rocks or sand, where it seldom rains in the north and never in the south, and the water they carry down from the mountains could only support small settlements near the mouths of the rivers until the cultivable area was extended by irrigation over large parts of the valley floors.

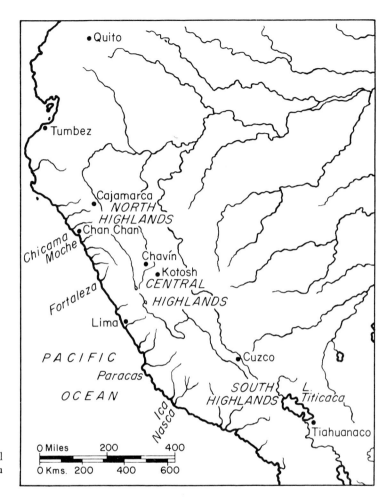

The temple at Kotosh, near Huánuco in the central
highlights, which has already been quoted as the oldest in
Peru, was embedded in a large mound where it was surrounded by the remains of other buildings, some at least
of which seem to have been ceremonial. The rectangular
temple, built of undressed stones set in mud mortar, with
plastered walls and floor, stood on a stepped platform
twenty-five feet high. The floor was surrounded by a
broad, low bench, and the interior walls had either
two or three tall rectangular niches in each. Below one

Ref. 7

Ill. 126

117

121 Warp striped cotton textile, with brocade cats. Chimú, North Coast. Fourteenth or fifteenth century A D

122 Spout-and-bridge effigy jar, showing a woman holding fruits, with a belt of monsters below. It illustrates the stylized modelling of the South Coast. Late Nasca. Probably seventh century A D

123, 124 Sculpture at Tiahuanaco, Bolivia. *Above*, the central figure on the monolithic doorway (*Ill. 133*), perhaps a sky god, holding staves representing spear-throwers and darts, which may typify thunderbolts. *Right*, a massive statue holding two beakers

125 The triple ramparts of the Inca fortress of Saccsai-huaman, overlooking Cuzco. Late fifteenth century AD

of these remained a pair of crossed hands modelled in the plaster, whence it has been called The Temple of the Crossed Hands. Llama bones were found in one of the niches, which is thought to show that they may already have been domesticated. Later, but still apparently before the introduction of pottery about 1800 B C, the temple was buried in boulders surrounded by a retaining wall and covered by a new floor on which a temple was built of which little remained. Like its predecessor, the floor was surrounded by a low bench, but in this case its outer edge had a series of deep, rectangular indentations. The burial of an old temple in the substructure of a later one is a foretaste of the widespread custom in Mesoamerica, but it is not known whether there was any connexion between them.

When agriculture began at Kotosh is not known, but the construction of massive platforms and temples implies a food surplus, of which the most probable source would have been root crops such as the potato, and perhaps Andean grains. Maize is thought to have been present by 1000 B C, but there is no reason to believe that it was an important food source even at that date.

The first pottery to appear at Kotosh, about 1800 B C, consists mainly of large neckless jars and bowls of various forms, with a great variety of incised geometrical decoration. It is mostly dark grey in colour, and what paint there is consists of red, with much less frequent yellow and white, applied to the incisions after firing. At several places on the coast, dark undecorated wares showing the marks of burnishing tools are found, and they are mostly bowls, large neckless jars of ovate profile, or globular jars with a low neck. The introduction of pottery to the coast is not exactly dated, but it was probably at about the same time as a low-yielding type of maize appeared, say 1400 to 1200 B C. Neither made much difference at first to the life of the coastal people. Although the first types of pottery to appear in both areas are simple and have early

126 The Temple of the Crossed Hands, Kotosh, Central Highlands of Peru, during excavation. Before 1800 B C

characteristics, the craft is unlikely to have been invented in Peru, since it appeared long before (about 3000 B C) in Ecuador and Colombia.

About 1000 B C began the Chavín horizon, which is marked by an art style which unites a large part of Peru. It is associated with the worship of a jaguar god, and the introduction of the loom and a new and more productive form of maize of undoubted Mesoamerican origin. Not only the maize but the jaguar cult and a number of pottery characteristics suggest a connexion with the Olmec culture of Mexico, and it has been suggested that these features may have been carried by a small group of immigrants. Some Chavínoid features appear a little earlier at Kotosh than the full Chavín horizon there, so there may

127, 128 North coast Peruvian pottery. *Left*, a spout-and-bridge whistling jar with monkey head, showing black negative painting on red. Vicus, far north of Peruvian coast. *Right*, three stirrup-spouted jars. Bottom left, dark grey ware, Coast Chavín. Top left, Mochica painted white, red and orange. Right, Chimú blackware

have been more than one migration, but the impact of the new arrivals appears less important than it did before the discovery of the much earlier temples at Kotosh. A few of the Mexican elements reached the coast of Ecuador, but the most conspicuous, including the jaguar cult, passed it by, so the migrations would probably have been by sea. After this time direct contacts between Mesoamerica and Peru ceased.

On the north coast the new arrivals seem to have taken control of the old inhabitants. They established new settlements away from the sea-shore, and perhaps began to develop irrigation. They built adobe temples to their feline god in several valleys. They introduced monochrome ceremonial pottery, some of which was realistically modelled to represent animals, human beings, vegetables and other life forms, a typical vessel being the

129 Temple at Chavín, North Highlands of Peru, showing a carved animal head tenoned into the masonry. The earliest stage is U-shaped and contains the prismatic granite idol. The temple was enlarged several times by adding rectangular blocks on either side. First millennium A D

stirrup-spouted jar, thus initiating a long-lived tradition on the north coast. Subsequently they began to work gold.

At Chavín, in the north highlands, they built a great *Ill. 129* platform-like temple, which has given its name to the horizon. It is built of regularly coursed masonry, honey-combed with passages, in one of which is an impressive idol in the form of a prismatic mass of granite carved in low relief to represent a human being with a jaguar head. Outside the temple are slabs and columns with carvings of jaguars and other beasts, birds and men, all related to the jaguar cult by their feline tusks, in many cases repeated on their bodies.

On the north coast, the coastal Chavín art style con-tinued until a date as yet undetermined, but probably in the last two centuries B C. Other styles appeared, such as Vicus which includes spout-and-bridge vessels possibly *Ill. 127* showing southern influence, but these seem to have been intrusions rather than members of the direct line of succession. The realistic modelling tradition was developed and refined, and a limited use of colour (typically white and red) was introduced, giving rise to the Mochica style. The stirrup spout continued but became lighter and underwent a series of changes in form, and many other vessel forms were made. Some pots were decorated with scenes in silhouette painting. In the meantime, maize farming resulted in a rapid increase in population and canal irrigation was developed. This resulted in the rise of states with centralized governments in the larger valleys, for irrigation in these circumstances is not possible without control. The greatest of these states, which, like its pottery style we call Mochica, spread by conquest from Moche and Chicama over a group of adjacent valleys, and became supreme in the north coast. It continued until about the end of the ninth century.

Ills 117, 119

Chavín art influenced a large part of the central coast as well as the north, and even affected the area round the Nasca and Ica Valleys in the south, which came to be the centre of a distinct artistic tradition. The influence of Chavín is estimated to have begun there between 700 and 600 B C, and have died away not later than 200 B C. It is seen chiefly in the depiction of jaguar faces on pottery and textiles. The southern artistic tradition was distinguished by the use of many colours rather than modelling for pottery decoration, and by an abundance of richly coloured and embroidered textiles lavished on the important dead, some of whom had artificially deformed skulls and some had been trephined several times during life. Among many pottery vessel forms, a very typical one is a closed jar with two narrow spouts, one of which may be replaced by a head or a figure, connected by a flat bridge, which takes the place of the stirrup-spout jar of the north. The subjects shown in the south are masked men, fantastic

Ill. 118

Ill. 132

130 South coast Peruvian pottery. Left, Paracas bowl with incised decoration, some post-fired painting and negative dot painting. Top right, double spout-and-bridge polychrome vessel, with monster above a band of trophy heads. Late Nasca. Bottom, black, white and red bowl with textile-derived patterns. Ica probably not long before the Inca conquest

composite monsters, and highly stylized animals, which show little interest in mundane matters, where as those of the north are naturalistic representations of everyday things. Until about the first century AD the pigments were applied to pottery as bright resinous colours after firing (the Paracas style), after which the potters had acquired sufficient skill to put a wide range of colours on before firing (the Nasca style), but they form a continuous succession. The tradition continued with minor stylistic changes until about AD 800.

Ill. 122

Other areas, such as the central coast and the north highlands, had their own styles, but the most conspicuous, of far-reaching importance, grew up in the south highlands. It is best known from developments at the great religious centre at Tiahuanaco on the bleak uplands near Lake Titicaca, where there is much skilfully worked masonry, the remains of a stone-faced pyramid, stairways and enclosures, also large, pillar-like statues and a carved monolithic doorway. The central figure shown on the doorway and features painted on the pottery are later found far afield, particularly representations of animals

Ill. 124
Ills 123, 133

125

131, 133 *Above*, Tiahuanaco pottery of three periods. Left, Early Tiahuanaco, feline effigy bowl, showing divided eyes. Centre, 'Classic' Tiahuanaco *kero*, or beaker. Right, decadent Tiahuanaco *kero* (later than AD 800). *Opposite*, the monolithic doorway at Tiahuanaco, showing three rows of running winged figures attending on the central one (*Ill. 123*)

132 Pottery from the Central Peruvian Coast, showing Highland influence from Tiahuanaco and Huari, resting on a contemporary tapestry with abstract designs which include divided eyes. The heads on the centre and left polychrome vessels, are derived from Tiahuanaco designs. The black, white and red head jar on the right is rather later

and birds with the eyes divided vertically into black and white halves.

The first eight centuries A D were a period of artistic and technological climax in all of the three main areas which have just been briefly surveyed, and it may be of interest to compare them with the Classic Maya period, which occupied very approximately the same span in Mesoamerica. In Peru there was no hieroglyphic writing and no evidence of an elaborate calendar, but on the other hand metals, gold, silver, copper, and their alloys had long been worked with great skill, while Mesoamerica was in the Stone Age. On the north coast of Peru conspicuous fortifications and representations of warriors on pottery show that militarism, on a scale comparable with that of the Toltecs, was rampant.

The key to what happened next is the Ayacucho region in the Mantaro Basin, where there is a large site called Huari, which was a cross-roads where influences, seen in the pottery, from Nasca and Tiahuanaco mingled with the local styles, and whence Tiahuanaco influences were passed on to Nasca. These influences are thought to have been religious, and are seen in the appearance of Tiahuanaco

Ill. 132

Ill. 134

Ill. 131

127

134 Unique Mochica gold puma skin of uncertain use, with repoussé decoration

Ill. 132

motifs on pottery and textiles. The most obvious are figures holding staves derived from the stone doorway, and animals, birds and human beings with divided eyes. Towards the end of the ninth century, there are signs of a great expansion from Huari, which can best be explained as military, affecting not only the Nasca area but the central coast and most of the central highlands. Pachacámac in the central coast, which became a famous oracle lasting until the Spaniards arrived, was established at this time. The climax was reached when the Mochica state was overrun early in the tenth century, and southern building plans as well as the southern custom of burial in mummy bundles were carried up to the Virú and Chicama Valleys. The Mochica art style was replaced by one influenced by Tiahuanaco, but it persisted in a modified form in the area of the Jequetepeque and Lambayeque Valleys in the far north. Highland rule reached its maximum extent by about AD 950.

This is one of the events which serve to knit together the many local developments in Peruvian archaeology, and it may be a parallel to the much later spread of the Inca. Each time, highlanders invaded the coast, and no cases of the contrary are known. There are great differences of altitude between the two regions, and adaptation from one to the other is a great strain, but the easier climatic conditions on the coast resulted in richer cultures, a likely attraction to the highlanders.

Shortly after they were established on the coast, the Tiahuanacoid art styles began to decay. Distinctive designs like the 'party-eyed' animals on pottery and textiles lost their character and disappeared, and the polychrome pottery bearing these designs gave place in time to a black, white and red style with geometrical decorations. There also appeared monochrome black or red wares bearing moulded ('pressed relief') designs, at first of Tiahuanaco derivation. Eventually three new states emerged in the north, central, and south parts of the coast. It was a time of political change, which witnessed the culmination of a process which began in the previous stage, namely the gathering of the people in large towns on a scale never attempted before. It is best seen in the northern state, the Chimú, called by the inhabitants Chimor, which was by far the largest and most powerful of the three, and it can be exemplified by its great mud-brick capital Chan-Chan, near Trujillo. This covers eleven square miles and contains ten great walled compounds, each like a city in miniature, separated from its fellows by irrigated areas, reservoirs and cemeteries. Each compound contains a palace-like structure and a pyramid, and is believed to have housed a clan or similar division under its chief, who thus had it under control. The largest of these towns were placed where the irrigation canals of two or more valleys could be fed in, giving rise to systems unprecedented in scale.

Ills 135, 136

Artistically it was a time of decadence. Each of the three states had its characteristic pottery style, but only that of the Chimú resembles that which existed before the highland invasion. It shares with its Mochica predecessor the use of elaborate modelling, and forms like the stirrup spout which go right through north coast prehistory, but it is carried out in black ware and the modelling is dull and lifeless. Pottery, textiles and metal work were all produced in large quantities, and decorated pots in particular were in general use instead of being made, as in the past, chiefly for the dead.

Ill. 128

The rise of the new states cannot have begun before about AD 1100 when the disintegration of the highland rule on the coast was far advanced, and the Chimú dynasty has been traced back to the early fourteenth century, so presumably this kingdom, and by analogy the other two, was taking shape, in the intervening two hundred years. By the middle of the fifteenth century the

Chimú king Minchançaman had conquered the coast from Tumbez in the north to the Fortaleza Valley in the south, and perhaps beyond it nearly to Lima.

In the highlands, the Inca dynasty and its subjects had been settled in and around Cuzco since about AD 1200. Like other small highland tribes they had engaged in raids and minor wars on their neighbours, but it was not until they had barely escaped a crushing defeat by the Chanca, another highland group, that they embarked on sustained conquests. These began with the accession to the throne in 1438 of Pachacuti, who had led their resistance to the Chanca. In the next twenty years he subdued the highlands from near Lake Titicaca in the south-east to Lake Junín in the north-west, and then his son, Topa Inca, was given command of the army and conquered the country up to Quito in the Ecuadorian Andes. Having overrun their highland allies in Cajamarca, he was in a strong position to attack the Chimú, since he commanded their water-supplies, and their great towns, whose food

135 Part of the great Chimú capital city of Chan-Chan, near Trujillo, north coast of Peru. It shows one of the great mud-brick compounds and parts of others, surrounded by high walls, probably built to control the inhabitants

136 Adobe (mud brick) building at Chan-Chan, north coast of Peru, the Chimú capital, showing stylized pelicans in relief. The designs are very similar to those on textiles and are clearly derived from them

supply was very vulnerable, were not adapted to threats from that quarter. Minchançaman resisted bitterly but in vain, his capital was looted, he was carried off to live in Cuzco, and one of his sons was installed in his place under Inca control. Subsequent conquests carried the Inca over the rest of the Peruvian coast, into north-west Argentina and down to Central Chile, and after Topa Inca's death in 1493 Huayna Capac conquered northern Ecuador, but none of these campaigns had an effect comparable with that of the conquest of the Chimú.

The Inca carried off much Chimú gold and other loot to Cuzco, also craftsmen from whom they learnt various textile and metal-working techniques, and mass-production methods especially of pottery. More important is the likelihood that much of the organization of the Empire was based on that of the Chimú, since it was not until after the conquest of the north coast that Topa Inca built it up in the form about which so much has been written. It was an impressive achievement, with its pyramidal

Ill. 137

137 Gold beaker with repoussé decoration and turquoise inlay. From the Lambayeque Valley, at the northern end of the Chimú domain and probably independent of it until the fifteenth century

138 Cuzco polychrome aryballus, the most characteristic Inca pottery shape. The larger ones were for carrying liquids on the back, but they were made in all sizes down to miniatures

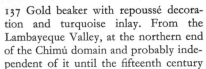
Ills 125, 139
Ill. 138

structure, its road system, and the integration of many peoples and customs, all accomplished by a people who had no means of writing and could only record figures on knotted strings. Witness to its greatness is borne not only by the Spanish chroniclers but also by its material remains, the great ruins of the Cuzco district and elsewhere, and the wide distribution of bronze tools and the Inca pottery style. If this had been built up from nothing in less than a century, it would have been scarcely credible, but the story needs qualification. The Inca system rose on the

139 Wall of the finest Inca masonry, originally part of the *accla huasi*, or ▷ House of the Chosen Women, Cuzco, who were dedicated to the service of the Inca and the temples. It is now a convent. The wall on the left is also Inca, so the street has its original width. Fifteenth century

foundation of earlier Peruvian civilizations, and most of its elements were not new. Stratified and specialist societies had long existed on the coast, and the Chimú are believed to have ruled through an hereditary aristocracy. On the material side they had, for example, a ready-made road system which the Inca took over. It is, moreover, unlikely that the organization was as standardized as is generally believed; a good instance is the retention by local coast chiefs of their ancestral lands when the standard Inca system was to divide all land between Emperor, religion and people. Nevertheless, when all allowances have been made, the Inca did a remarkable thing in uniting such an enormous and diversified area, organizing its communications and supplies and building up rank upon rank of officials, each responsible to the Emperor through his representative in the rank above.

The Empire was a despotism, with an absolute, divine ruler supported by an hereditary aristocracy, but the well-being of its subjects was in the interests of both. The measures taken to ensure this have given rise to the idea that it was a sort of socialistic welfare state, but states of that sort do not move unruly tribes forcibly from their homes to live among docile peoples and send loyal *mitimaes* to take their place, neither do they have one law for the nobles and another for commoners as the Inca did. The lands of the peasant group or *ayllu* were held in common and redistributed among its members each year; this feature, at the agricultural base of the Inca pyramid, was doubtless very ancient, but it was the only egalitarian or theoretically communistic characteristic of the system. There is in fact little profit in comparing the Inca Empire to modern political structures.

The success of the Inca armies cannot be ascribed to superior arms because they fought with the same weapons as their enemies, but a large factor must have been the sustained aggressiveness, which contrasts with the general highland custom of short-lived raids. This was backed by their organizing ability, which enabled them to raise and maintain armed levies, to supply them from their store-houses, and to move them rapidly along their roads to where they wished. Many of their conquests were accomplished by threats and diplomacy, and their fiercest battles were with comparatively small highland tribes like the Cañari of Ecuador.

The persistence of the offensive spirit is doubtless to be ascribed to various motives. The first conquests after the Chanca defeat may well have been undertaken to secure the Inca position, but the consequent increase of power and wealth seem to have bred the taste for more. The aristocracy was polygamous and increased rapidly, and its young men were nurtured in the arts of war. A campaign gave an outlet for their energies, and subsequently provided some with responsible posts in conquered territory. There seem to have been some signs of unrest among the ruling classes, possibly owing to unsatisfied ambition and idleness, a potential source of weakness. The Empire was still in a state of active development when the Spaniards landed in 1532, and what its subsequent history would have been is a matter for speculation. Two main factors undermined its strength. One was the lack of a fixed rule of succession among the Emperor's sons, which resulted in the civil war between Huascar and Atahuallpa when Huayna Capac died before deciding who should succeed him. The other was inherent in the structure itself; all owed allegiance to the Emperor at the head of the pyramid, but there was insufficient cohesion at each level of society. While the Emperor was venerated as a divine monarch this was no weakness, but when a handful of invaders, who cared for none of these things, struck at Atahuallpa, the head and heart of the Empire, they brought it to the dust.

Bibliography

1 Works covering a wide area

WILLEY, G. R., *An Introduction to American Archaeology*. Vol. 1, *North and Middle America*. New Jersey, 1966. A modern archaeological textbook with a full bibliography. Vol. 2 will cover Central and South America.

WAUCHOPE, ROBERT, editor, *Handbook of Middle American Indians*. Vols. 1–3. London, 1964–5. This will be completed in 11 volumes.

STEWARD, JULIAN H., editor, *Handbook of South American Indians*. 7 volumes. Washington, 1946–57. Partly out of date, but still useful.

2 Works covering more limited areas

BUSHNELL, G. H. S., *Peru*. 2nd ed. London, 1963.

COE, M. D., *Mexico*. London, 1962.

—— *The Maya*. London, 1966.

MEGGERS, B. J., *Ecuador*. London, 1966.

MORLEY, S. J., and BRAINERD, G. W., *The Ancient Maya*. 3rd ed. Stanford, 1956.

REICHEL-DOLMATOFF, G., *Columbia*. London, 1965.

ROUSE, I., and CRUXENT, J. M., *Venezuelan Archaeology*. London (Yale U.P.), 1963.

THOMPSON, J. E. S., *The Rise and Fall of Maya Civilization*. 2nd ed. Norman, Oklahoma, 1966.

3 References

1. WENDORF, F., Early Man in the New World: Problems of Migration. *The American Naturalist*. Vol. 100, No. 912. May–June 1966, p. 253.
2. WORMINGTON, H. M., *Ancient Man in North America*. 4th ed. Denver, Colorado, 1957.
3. LANNING, E. P., Early Man in Peru. *Scientific American*. October 1965, p. 68.
4. MACNEISH, R. S., *Tehuacán Archaeological-Botanical Project, First and Second Annual Reports*. Andover, Mass., 1961, 2.
5. ENGEL, F., El Precerámico sin Algodón en la Costa del Peru. *XXXV Congreso Internacional de Americanistas, Mexico 1962. Actas y Memorias, 3*, p. 141.
6. DONNAN, C. B., An Early House from Chilca, Peru. *American Antiquity*, Vol. 30, No. 2, Part 1, October 1964, p. 137.
7. IZUMI, S., and SONO, T., *Andes 2. Excavations at Kotosh, Peru, 1960*. Tokyo, 1963.
8. LATHRAP, D. W., Origins of Central Andean Civilization: New Evidence. *Science*. Vol. 148, 7 May 1965, pp. 796–8.
9. COE, M. D., *et al.*, Olmec Civilization, Veracruz, Mexico: Dating of the San Lorenzo Phase. *Science*. Vol. 155, 17 March 1967, p. 1399.
10. GAY, C. T. E., Oldest Paintings of the New World. *Natural History*, LXXVI, No. 4. April 1967, p. 28.
11. COE, M. D., *The Jaguar's Children: Pre-Classic Central Mexico*. New York, 1965.
12. —— The Chinampas of Mexico. *Scientific American*. July 1964, p. 90.
13. Articles in *Handbook of South American Indians* (see above, section 1), Vol. 4.
14. MCGIMSEY, C. R. III, Cerro Mangote. A Preceramic Site in Panama. *American Antiquity*. Vol. 22, No. 2, p. 151.
15. LANNING, E. P., Current Research in Highland South America. *American Antiquity*. Vol. 31, No. 1, July 1965, p. 139, also personal communication.
16. COE, M. D., and BAUDEZ, C. F., The Zoned Bichrome Period in North-Western Costa Rica. *American Antiquity*. Vol. 26, No. 4, April 1961, p. 505.

List of Illustrations

The author and publishers are grateful to the many official bodies, institutions and individuals mentioned below for their assistance in supplying illustration material. Illustrations without acknowledgement are from originals in the archives of Thames and Hudson. Objects in the University Museum of Archaeology and Ethnology, Cambridge are designated CMAE and are reproduced from Museum photographs with permission. MNAM—Museo Nacional de Antropologiá, Mexico D.F.

Chronological Table drawn by Lucinda Rodd after the author

137

19 Pottery figure of a baby, Tlatilco, Valley of Mexico. Private collection, Mexico D. F. Photo Irmgard Groth-Kimball

20 Jade celt. Olmec Culture, British Museum. Photo John Webb

21 Fish-shaped bowl, Tlatilco, Valley of Mexico. MNAM. Photo Irmgard Groth-Kimball

22 Bowl, Tlatilco, Valley of Mexico. CMAE

23 Pottery mask, Tlatilco, Valley of Mexico. Private Collection. Photo Irmgard Groth-Kimball

24 Pottery female figure with two heads, Tlatilco, Valley of Mexico. Private collection. Photo Irmgard Groth-Kimball

25 Map of Mesoamerica and Central America. Drawn by Shalom Schotten

26 Monte Albán, Oaxaca, Mexico. Photo R. B. Welsh

27 Carved sandstone revetment slabs. Monte Albán, Oaxaca. Photo T. G. Rosenthal

28 Pottery funerary urn in the form of Cocijo, the rain god. Zapotec, Oaxaca. CMAE

29 Map of Maya sites in South Mexico and Guatemala. Drawn by Charles Hasler

30 Temple 1, Tikal, Guatemala. Photo the author

31 Green jade, Teotihuacán, Mexico. British Museum. Photo Eileen Tweedy

32 Jade flare, Pomona, British Honduras. British Museum. Photo Eileen Tweedy

33 Room 1, Structure 1, Bonampak, Chiapas, Mexico. Drawn by Martin Weaver after Tullock

34 Painting with musicians, Bonampak, Chiapas. Copy by Antonio Tejeda, courtesy of the Carnegie Institution, Washington

35 Painting in Room 2, Structure 1, Bonampak, Chiapas. Copy by Antonio Tejeda, courtesy of the Carnegie Institution, Washington

36 Maya stucco head from the Temple of the Inscriptions burial chamber, Palenque, Chiapas, Mexico. NNAM. Photo Irmgard Groth-Kimball

37, 38 Sections of the Temple of the Inscriptions, Palenque, Chiapas. Drawn by Peter Pratt after Ruz

39 Burial chamber, Temple of the Inscriptions, Palenque, Chiapas. Photo courtesy of Dr Alberto Ruz

40 Corbelled and true arches. Drawn by Martin Weaver

41 Temple of the Sun, Palenque, Chiapas. Photo courtesy of the American Museum of Natural History, New York

42 Page from the Dresden Codex. Staatsbibliothek, Dresden

43 Reconstruction of the site of Copán. Photo courtesy of the Peabody Museum, Harvard University

44 Stela B, Copán. Photo A. P. Maudslay, courtesy of the Trustees of the British Museum

45 Itzamná the fire god. Drawn from the Dresden Codex by Hubert Pepper

46 Chac the rain god. Drawn from the Dresden Codex by Hubert Pepper

75 *Cenote*, Chichén Itzá, Yucatán

76 Group of the Columns, Mitla. Oaxaca, Mexico. Photo T. G. Rosenthal

77 Stone mosaic, Mitla. Photo T. G. Rosenthal

78, 79 Mixtec tripod bowls, Oaxaca, Mexico. CMAE

80, 81 Cup and bowl, Cholula Ware. CMAE

82 Gold pendant from Tomb 7, Monte Albán, Oaxaca. NMAM. Photo Irmgard Groth-Kimball

83, 84 Folios 16 and 17, Codex Nuttall. British Museum. Photos courtesy of the Trustees of the British Museum

85 Tlateloco pyramid, Mexico. Photo the author

86 Feathered serpent, Quetzalcóatl. NMAM

87 Quetzalcóatl and Tlaloc, from the Codex Magliabecchi. Biblioteca Nazionale Centrale, Florence. Drawn by Diana Holmes

88 Head of an Eagle Knight wearing an eagle helmet. NMAM

89 Wooden war drum, Malinalco. NMAM

90 Spear-thrower, Valley of Mexico. British Museum. Photo John Freeman

91 Sacrificial knife with inlaid handle in the form of a crouching Eagle Knight. Tenochtitlán, Valley of Mexico. British Museum. Photo courtesy of the Trustees of the British Museum

92 Painting of human sacrifice, Temple of Jaguars, Chichén Itzá, Yucatán. Drawn by Hubert Pepper after Morley

93 Pottery flute, Valley of Mexico. CMAE

94 God on pyramid, Valley of Mexico. CMAE

95 Stone Xipe mask, back view with priest. British Museum. Photo Edwin Smith

96 Stone Xipe mask. British Museum. Photo courtesy of the Trustees of the British Museum

97 Feather head-dress given to Cortés by Moctezuma II. Museum für Völkerkunde, Vienna

98 Aztec feather shield. Museum für Völkerkunde, Vienna. Photo courtesy Conzett and Huber, Zürich

99 Mosaic mask based on a human skull British Museum. Photo courtesy of the Trustees of the British Museum

100 Carved stone of King Tizoc from main temple enclosure at Tenochtitlán, Valley of Mexico

101 Aztec pottery. CMAE

102 Colima, Mexico, 'dancing' dogs. Original NNAM, photo from a cast

103 Colima figure of a man blowing a conch-shell trumpet. Arensberg Collection, Philadelphia Museum of Art

104 Valdivia tetrapod bowl, Ecuador. Photo Clifford Evans

105 Stone grinding-slab, Costa Rica. Private collection

106 Polychrome bottle, Coclé, Panamà. CMAE

107 Chibcha anthropomorphic vase, Colombia. Museo Nacional, Bogotá

108 Grotesque statue, San Augustín, North Mound of Mesita B, Columbia. Photo Instituto Colombiano de Antropologiá

109 Grotesque stone statue, Costa Rica, Private collection

110 Chibcha double vessel with bridge. Drawn by Pauline Bright

111 Valdivia pottery female figurine, Ecuador. Photo Clifford Evans

112 Objects of precious metal from Quimbaya, Cauca Valley. Colombia. British Museum. Photo courtesy of the Trustees of the British Museum

113 Chibcha wedge-shaped gold figurine, Colombia. Museo del Oro, Bogotá

114 La Plata seated type hollow figurine, Colombia. Photo Clifford Evans

115 Pottery head-rest with double column support. Photo Clifford Evans

116 Chimney burial in mound on the Babahoyo river, Ecuador. Photo Clifford Evans

117 Mochica stirrup-spouted jar, Peru. CMAE

118 Lay figure wearing textiles from a Paracas mummy. National Museum, Lima. Photo courtesy of Dr Jorge Muelle

119 Stirrup-spouted jar, *left*, North Coast, Peru; polychrome jar, *below*, South Coast, Peru; jar, *right*, North Highlands, Peru. All on ancient textile. CMAE

120 Map of Peru drawn by Lucinda Rodd

121 Chimú textile with pattern of brocaded cats, Peru. CMAE

122 Nasca spout-and-bridge effigy jar, Peru. CMAE

123 Detail of the central figure on the main gateway, Tiahuanaco, Bolivia. Photo R. B. Welsh

124 Monolithic statue of a god or warrior, Tiahuanaco. Photo R. B. Welsh

125 Saccsaihuaman fort near Cuzco, Peru. Photo R. B. Welsh

126 Temple at Kotosh, Peru. Photo courtesy of Professor Kazuo Terada

127 Vicus spout-and-bridge jar, Peru. CMAE

128 Chavín, Mochica and Chimú jars, North Coast, Peru. CMAE

129 Rear of the temple at Chavin, Peru. Photo R. B. Welsh

130 Painted pottery, South Coast, Peru. CMAE

131 Highland Tiahuanaco pottery, Bolivia. CMAE

132 Coastal Tiahuanaco pottery on contemporary textile, Peru. CMAE

133 Main gateway, Tiahuanaco. Photo courtesy of the Director, Museo Nacional, Tiahuanaco, Bolivia

134 Gold repoussé puma skin, Mochica, Peru. M. Mugica Gallo collection. Photo John Webb

135 Air view of Chan-Chan, Peru. Photo courtesy of the American Geographical Society

136 Detail of pelicans in textile style design. Chan-Chan. Photo R. B. Welsh

137 Repoussé gold beaker, Lambayeque, Peru. M. Mugica Gallo collection. Photo John Webb

138 Inca aryballus, Cuzco, Peru. CMAE

139 Inca wall, Cuzco, Peru. Photo H. Mann

141

Index

Numbers in italics refer to illustrations